HEINEMANN

SECONDARY

HISTORY

PROJECT

THE AMERICAN WEST

Susan Willoughby

Head of History, Hodgson High School, Poulton-le-Fylde

Heinemann

Heinemann Educational Publishers
Halley Court, Jordan Hill, Oxford OX2 8EJ
a division of Reed Educational and Professional
Publishing Ltd

MELBOURNE AUCKLAND FLORENCE PRAGUE MADRID
ATHENS SINGAPORE KUALA LUMPUR TOKYO
SAO PAULO CHICAGO PORTSMOUTH NH (USA)
MEXICO CITY IBADAN GABORONE JOHANNESBURG
KAMPALA NAIROBI

First Published 1996

99 98 97 96
10 9 8 7 6 5 4 3 2 1

British Library Cataloguing in Publication Data is
available from the British Library on request.

ISBN 0 435 30921 8

Produced by Visual Image, Street, Somerset
Illustrated by Visual Image, Jane Watkins
Printed by Mateu Cromo in Spain
Cover design by The Wooden Ark Studio
Cover photo: *A Group of Sioux* by Charles Deas, 1845.
Reproduced by permission of the Amon Carter Museum, Fort
Worth, Texas.

This book is for Andrew, David and Helen and all the other
youngsters of Hodgson High School who have, at some time,
travelled along this trail.

Acknowledgements
The publishers would like to thank the following for
permission to reproduce photographs:

American Heritage Center, University of Wyoming: 74 below,
77 below, 80 centre below; Arizona Historical Society, Tucson:
74 top left; Art Resource, New York/National Museum of
American Art, Washington: 17; Baker Library, Harvard
Business School: 64; Bancroft Library, University of California,
Berkeley: 34; Buffalo Bill Historical Center, Cody, Wyoming:
21 / Gift of Mrs J Maxwell Moran 11/ Werner Forman
Archive: 23/ Gift of Barbara S Leggett: 54; / Gertrude
Vanderbilt Whitney Trust Fund purchase: 93 top;/ Gift of
William E. Weiss: 18, 20; Butler Institute of American Art,
Youngstown, Ohio: 31; Colorado Historical Society: 87;
Denver Public Library, Western History Department: 8, 45, 60;
Mary Evans Picture Library: 36, 39; Gilcrease Museum, Tulsa,
Oklahoma: 46, 50, 58; Joslyn Art Museum, Omaha: 19; Kansas
State Historical Society, Topeka: 29, 44, 52 below, 67, 74 top
right; Mansell Collection: 26, 38; Montana Historical Society,
Helena: 76; Nebraska State Historical Society: 66; Peter
Newark's Western Americana: 5, 24, 33, 47, 52 top, center, 53,
55, 56, 61, 71, 73, 78, 80 top, 83, 89, 91, 93 below; Oxford
Scientific Films/ Roland Mayr: 16; South Dakota State
Historical Society, Pierre, South Dakota: 10; Warner Bros
(courtesy John Kobel Collection): 4; Western History
Collections, University of Oklahoma Library: 70, 77 top left,
right, 79;

The publishers have made every effort to trace copyright
holders of material in this book. Any omissions will be
rectified in subsequent printings if notice is given to the
publisher.

E.C. Abbott, *We Pointed them North*, University of Oklahoma
    Press 1966: 5.3C
Ralf K. Andrist, (quoted in) *The Long Death,* Macmillan
    Company (New York) 1964: 8.1A, 8.2A - M
J.I.H. Baur (ed.), *Autobiography of Worthington Whittredge*,
    Brooklyn Museum Journal, 1842: 1.2B
S.M. Barret (ed.), *Geronimo, his own Story*, Abacus, Sphere
    Books, 1974: 2.3F
Dee Brown, *Bury My Heart at Wounded Knee*, Holt, Rinehart
    and Winston, 1971: 8.3A
George Catlin, *Manners, Customs and Condition of the North
    American Indians, Vol 1*, Dover Publications Inc, New York,
    1844: 2.1B, 2.3D, 2.3G, 2.4A, 2.4D; Vol II, 2.5A
William Clayton, *A Daily Record of the Journey of The Original
    company of Mormon Pioneers from Nauvoo to the Valley of the
    Great Salt Lake*, Salt Lake City, 1921: 3.3F
Henry Commager, (ed.) (quoted in) *The West*, Orbis
    Publishing Co, 1976: Page 29, 3.2A, B, C, D, 4.1F, 6.1, B, C,
    D, 6.3B, D
Early Western Travel Series, Vol xvii, Arthur H. Clark and
    Company, 1904: 1.2A
J. Evetts Haley, Charles Goodnight: Cowman and Plainsman,
    University of Oklahoma Press, 1949: 5.3F, 5.3H
Odie B. Faulk, *The Crimson Desert*, OUP, 1974: 2.5C
J.G. Fraser, *The Native Races of America*, Lund Humphries,
    1939: 2.4B
W. Grasswasking, *Proceedings of Denver County Court*, Frink,
    Jackson and Spring, University of Colorado Press, 1956:
    5.2D
E.A. Hoebel, *The Cheyenne*, Holt, Rinehart and Winston, 1978:
    2.5B
Royal B. Hassrick, *The American West*, Octopus Books Ltd,
    1975: 5.3E
Luther Standing Bear, *My People the Sioux*, University of
    Nebraska Press, 1975: 2.1A, 2.4E
Robin May, (quoted in) *History of the American West*, Hamlyn,
    1984: 4.1C, 5.3E
Robin May, (quoted in) *The Story of the Wild West*, Hamlyn,
    1978: 7.1B, 7.1C, D, G, H
Joseph McCoy, *Historic Sketches of the Cattle Trade of the West
    and South West*, Kansas City, Missouri: 5.3I
Clyde A. Milner, Carol A. O'Connor, Martha A. Sandweiss
    (eds.) *The Oxford History of the American West*, OUP, 1994:
    1.3A, 1.4A, 1.4B, 5.1A
W. Mulder and A.R. Mortensen, *Amongst the Mormons*, Alfred
    A. Knopf, 1958: 3.3B
J. Neihardt (ed.), *Black Elk Speaks*. Spere Books, 1974: 2.2D
Francis Parkman, *The Oregon Trail*, 1847: 2.3C
Schools Council History 13-16 Project, (quoted in) *The
    American West 1840-95*, Holmes, McDougall, 1977: 3.1F, G,
    5.2E, 5.3H, 7.1E, 7.1G
O.D. Winter, (ed.) *A Friend of the Mormons, Thomas L Kane*, San
    Francisco, Calfornia, 1937: 3.1E

The Publishers would like to thank John Browning and Mike
McIntyre for their comments on the original manuscript.

CONTENTS

CHAPTER 1

FANTASY, FACTS AND FRONTIERS

The stranger rides into town. No one knows who he is but he looks like trouble. Rumours fly as he heads for the saloon. The good-time girls eye him with interest. The gamblers fall silent at their tables. The stranger downs his drink and slowly turns. Another drinker rises to face him. 'This town,' he spits, 'ain't big enough for the both of us.' They go for their guns . . .

▲ **A scene from the film *Wyatt Earp*, 1994.**

'Western' books and films have been popular for decades: cowboys and Indians, gunslingers and cattle-rustlers. Many of these stories are pure fantasy, but some of their characters and settings are drawn from true history. You might have heard of Wyatt Earp, Billy the Kid, Sitting Bull, Jesse James and Geronimo. They were all real people, living in an important and exciting period in the development of the USA – 1840 to 1895. Between those years the great expanse of the American West was won by white people – and lost by the Indians who were already living there.

This first chapter will give an overview of the main groups of people involved in the winning and losing of the West. To start with it is important to understand the history and the geography of the North American continent.

1.1 America - the beginning

In 1492 Christopher Columbus sailed west from Europe with the aim of reaching India. Instead he found himself among the native people of an unexpected continent: America. He still called these people Indians and the name remained. 'There is not in the world a better nation,' he wrote to the King and Queen of Spain. 'Their manners are decorous [correct] and praiseworthy.'

These Indians lived in many tribes. They were not one 'nation', as they were descended from the peoples who migrated from Siberia, Asia and northern China at a time,

CANADA
ruled by Britain

OREGON
TERRITORY
bought from
Britain 1846

Given up by Britain 1818

LOUISIANA
PURCHASE
from France
1803

From Mexico after
war 1848

Missouri River

UNITED
STATES
by 1800

Given up by
Mexico 1848

Arkansas River

Mississippi River

Red River

THIRTEEN ORIGINAL STATES
The USA (1783)

*Pacific
Ocean*

Bought from
Mexico 1853

TEXAS
independent
until 1845

Rio Grande

MEXICO

FLORIDA
bought from
Spain 1810-19

*Atlantic

Ocean*

Gulf of Mexico

0   500 Miles
0   800 km

Great Lakes

N

▲ **The growth of the United States of America 1783–1853.**

thousands of years ago, when Alaska and Siberia were joined by land. Over the next two centuries Britain, France and Spain established empires in the Americas. In 1775 the settlers in thirteen east coast colonies rebelled against their British rulers, and won the **War of Independence** that followed. Thus, in 1783, the republic of the **United States of America** was born.

What was the 'West'?

The West was whatever lay beyond the USA's western frontier – the boundary of the land that was settled and inhabited by white Americans. In 1783 it lay along the Appalachian Mountains, but this boundary was to change many times until, by 1895, a single frontier line was no longer visible. The map above shows how, after 1800, the US Government gradually acquired all the land from the Atlantic to the Pacific – by purchase, by war, or by negotiation.

▶ **Sitting Bull, a famous chief of the Sioux tribe who resisted the attempts of the US government to confine the Plains Indians to reservations in the 1860s and 1870s. He and another Sioux chief, Crazy Horse, fought against General Custer at the battle of the Little Bighorn in 1876 (see chapter 8).**

The map (right) shows the main physical features of the United States as it exists today. It covers an enormous area of land – five times greater than that of Great Britain, France, Germany and Japan combined. At first, the earliest European settlers clung to the eastern coastal region, rarely venturing beyond the Appalachian Mountains. They knew little of the fertile farmlands of the Mississippi River valley, or of the vast, desert-like territories that rolled westward on its far side. The two maps describe these lands from the East coast to the Pacific ocean.

Into the Great American Desert

In the heart of North America is a massive area of grassland known today as the Great Plains. In the eastern part of the Plains, the land is flat with long prairie grass as far as the eye can see. Moving westwards, the grass becomes shorter as the land rises to the foothills of the Rocky Mountains. Nineteenth-century schoolbooks described this area as the **Great American Desert**: it was said to be a mostly barren land with a hostile climate that would not be suitable for successful farming.

As the map shows, the Plains are crossed by a number of rivers, yet conditions in the south really are desert-like. Everywhere the wind howls constantly – burning the skin and drying the land in summer, carrying blizzards and the freezing cold in winter.

Beyond the Plains

The Plains are bounded in the west by the Rocky Mountains. In the south the Rockies are heavily wooded. Grizzly bears, beavers and mountain lions once roamed there, attracting hardy hunters and trappers. Moving westwards, the land descends from the Rockies to the plateaux region. This was another area of semi-desert vegetation (sagebrush and cacti) and dry, hostile winds. To the north of this region lies the Columbia Plateau. Lying lower in the centre is the Great Basin which includes the Great Salt Lake. Further south the Colorado River Plateau is an area of dramatic canyons and ravines.

The Sierra Nevada and the Pacific coastlands

The snow-capped peaks of the Sierra Nevada form the backbone of the Pacific coastlands and rise from the western edge of the Plateaux region. Their slopes are thickly wooded and reach, in places, a height of 4,500 metres. In contrast to the Plains and the Plateaux, the Pacific coastlands (the states of California and Oregon) are more hospitable with a milder climate and fertile soils.

Source B

Whoever crossed the Plains at that period, notwithstanding its herds of buffalo and flocks of antelope, its wild horses, deer and fleet rabbits, could hardly fail to be impressed with its vastness and silence and the appearance everywhere of an innocent primitive existence.

▲ From the *Autobiography of Worthington Whitteredge*, published in the *Brooklyn Museum Journal*, 1842.

QUESTION

1 If you had been considering moving West in the 1840s to farm what practical problems might you have encountered?

Source A

In regard to this extensive section of country, I do not hesitate in giving the opinion, that it is almost wholly unfit for cultivation, and of course uninhabitable by a people depending upon agriculture for their subsistence . . . the scarcity of wood and water will prove an insuperable obstacle in the way of settling in the West.

▲ A description of the Great Plains by Major Stephen Long, 1819–20.

CANADA

OREGON

Cascades

Columbia
Plateau

Rocky Mountains

Great Lakes

CALIFORNIA

Sierra Nevada

Great
Basin

**Great
Salt Lake**

Colorado
Plateau

Great Plains

Missouri River

Arkansas River

Mississippi River

Red River

Appalachian Mountains

N

*Pacific
Ocean*

Rio Grande

MEXICO

Gulf of Mexico

*Atlantic
Ocean*

500 Miles

0

800 km

0

	Eastern lowlands.

Low Plains
(long prairie grass)

High Plains
(short grass)

} The Great Plains –
called the Great
American Desert
due to continous
winds and extremes
of hot and cold.

The Rocky Mountains. Heavily wooded in the South, home to
grizzly bears and beavers.
The Plateau Region – Columbia Plateau, semi-desert.
The Great Basin – very dry, includes the Great Salt Lake.
Colorado River Plateau – canyons and deep ravines.
Sierra Nevada – high, forested mountain range forming a
barrier between the Plains and the Pacific coastlands.

Pacific coastlands – *California* and *Oregon*. Warm and fertile.

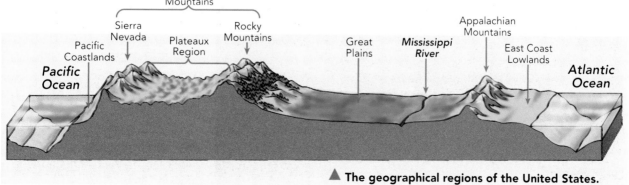

Mountains

Sierra
Nevada

Plateaux
Region

Rocky
Mountains

Great
Plains

*Mississippi
River*

Appalachian
Mountains

Pacific
Coastlands

East Coast
Lowlands

*Pacific
Ocean*

*Atlantic
Ocean*

▲ **The geographical regions of the United States.**

The story of the West was one of constant movement – some settlers going out, others returning, some following later to join friends or relatives, some (especially the Indians) being forced to move on as others 'invaded' lands which they regarded as their own. As you will see, both fair means and foul were used in the opening up of the new territories.

Who were the American pioneers?

A pioneer is someone who blazes a trail where others might one day follow. After hearing from mountain men and trappers about distant fertile lands, farming families in Missouri or Arkansas for example, who could not find land and were short of money, started to head for Oregon (see map opposite) in the early 1840s. By 1845 there were about 6,000 of these settlers living in Oregon. At that time, ownership of Oregon was shared between Great Britain and the USA, but in 1846, after long negotiations, the USA aquired the whole state.

Who went to California – and why?

The Pacific territory of California was less attractive to settlers from the East. It was much harder to reach because less was known about the trails that led there. In addition, until 1848 it belonged to Mexico. But in January of that year the USA won it after a war with the Mexicans. The timing could not have been better. Just eight days before peace was signed, gold was discovered in the foothills of the Sierra Nevada. This started a 'rush' of an estimated 90,000 gold prospectors by 1849.

Source A

American and European migrants farming land to the west of the Appalachian Mountains 1800-1910:

1800	450,000
1850	1,500,000
1910	6,400,000

▲ These figures are taken from the official US Census. It is interesting to note that in 1850 only 119,000 of these migrants were located west of the Mississippi River.

Mining camps – and later mining towns – attracted all kinds of people, some of whom were dishonest and unruly. Later discoveries of gold drew prospectors to Idaho, Montana and Arizona (in the early 1860s) and Dakota (in 1874). All these farmers and gold miners were pioneers – the first to struggle in their covered wagons along the Plains routes and over the mountains.

Source B

◀ A Mormon family, pictured with handcarts on the trail in northern Utah in 1867.

The Mormons

The **Saints** were also pioneers. They were members of a religious sect – the Church of Jesus Christ of the Latter Day Saints, or **Mormons** as they became more commonly known. To escape persecution for their religious beliefs and way of life, they trekked westwards in 1847, finally settling in the plateaux region near the Great Salt Lake. They turned the barren wasteland they found there into a fertile farming region. They founded Salt Lake City and, eventually, the prosperous state of Utah.

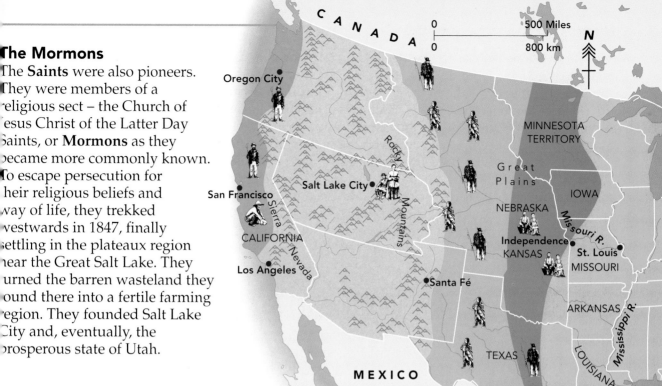

▲ The first settlers in the West in the late 1840s and the 1850s.

Homesteaders, cattlemen and cowboys

By the 1860s the myth of the Great American Desert (see map page 7) was seen to be false as settlers began to take up the challenge of making a living on the Great Plains. Between 1854 and 1865 the first **homesteaders** (farmers) began to move on to the eastern prairie lands of the Plains into the territories of Kansas and Nebraska. Some were from the East and some were former Negro slaves who had been freed in 1865. But from the 1860s onwards, more and more foreign immigrants, mainly from Europe, went to the American West in search of a better life. They were helped on their way by the completion of a railway right across America in 1869.

Key:
- Cattlemen
- Farmers
- Homesteaders
- Gold diggers
- Mormons
- Indians
- Indian reservations
- ——— Old "permanent Indian frontier"

▲ The extent of settlement in the West by 1895.

Almost at the same time as the homesteaders came onto the Plains from the East, the **cattlemen** began to cross the Plains from the south (look at the map on page 51). Each summer, from 1866 onwards, enterprising cattlemen from Texas employed cowboys to drive herds of several hundred head of Texas Longhorns across the Plains, northwards to meet the railway. Cattle towns such as Dodge City, Abilene, Ellsworth, Wichita and Sedalia sprang up along the railway. Here cattle were bought and sold for a good price, and then transported to the cities of the East and the mining towns of the West. The cattle business boomed from the late 1860s to the mid-1880s. During the 1870s more and more cattlemen began to establish ranches on the Plains. This led to conflict between the cattlemen and the homesteaders. The Longhorns grazed freely on the **open range** and frequently roamed on to the land cultivated by the homesteaders and damaged or destroyed their crops.

1.4 What did the West have to offer?

(look at the map on page 51)

Source A

▲ A poster published by South Dakota to attract settlers.

Land in the East was expensive, especially for people like the Irish immigrants who began to arrive in America in great numbers in the late 1840s. In the West, by contrast, there was plenty of land that could be free, cheap, or bought on easy terms at low rates of interest. Much of the Plains land was made available on these terms by the railway companies. They had been given large tracts of land by the US Government as a means of raising the funds to build the railway.

Some people left the East because they saw the West as a **land of opportunity** – and not just for farmers. Letters and newspaper articles inspired business people, teachers, churchmen, lawyers and would-be politicians to go and practise their skills in the new settlements and communities. Others still were driven there for **religious** reasons.

Source B

Up to and including 1880 the country had a frontier [boundary] of settlement, but at present the unsettled area has been so broken into by isolated bodies of settlement that there can hardly be said to be a frontier line.

▲ Extract from the official census report of 1890.

As well as the Mormons, many of the persecuted peoples of Europe migrated to the American West.

How did the authorities help?

Once settlement had begun, some territorial governments made deliberate efforts to encourage further migration. In 1855, for example, the territory of Minnesota set up a **Board of Immigration** to attract more settlers.

The US Government also played a key role. It was important that all the USA's territory should be occupied by American citizens, and legislation like the 1862 Homestead Act (see page 64) encouraged migration by allowing land to be bought at low prices. The Government also published maps and reports and provided protection for travellers by sending units of the US Army to the West.

So plenty of people back East were making sure that the West would be won and kept. Some of them came to see this as the nation's destiny....

What was manifest destiny?

There was a belief, first expressed publicly in 1845 that white American people were destined to occupy and govern all the territories of North America. It was very strongly held, particularly by politicians in the capital city of Washington.

This belief encouraged and justified their efforts to gain land from, for example, Mexico and Britain. It also encouraged the migration of settlers, and helped people with a conscience to come to terms with taking land from the Plains Indians.

In 1834 an Indian frontier had been guaranteed by the US Government. This followed a north-south line along the eastern edge of the Great Plains. But soon white Americans were overstepping it. The migration of so many 'pale faces' naturally affected the Indian way of life. It also meant that the gradual formation of territories and the need of government control led to the establishment of federal government, and we will now look at the constitution of the United States.

Source C

. . . the fulfilment of our manifest destiny to overspread the continent allotted by Providence for the free development of our yearly multiplying millions.

▲ **John L. O'Sullivan, editor of the** *Democratic Revue*, **July 1845.**

Source D

▲ A painting by William Ranney called *Advice on the Prairie* (1853). In the early 1850s, when mass migration on to the Plains had just begun, settlers travelled in family groups in a covered wagon.

America is governed under rules set out in the **Constitution of the United States**. This was drawn up in 1787 after the thirteen original colonies on the east coast had won their independence from Britain. At first it only applied to these states and was designed to protect their interests.

However, the new areas that were becoming inhabited needed some organization and government. At first, the US government called these lands **public domain** but when settlers began to move West, the areas in which they settled became known as **federal territories**. The government in Washington sent out officials, chosen by the President, to govern these territories. As the population grew, they were allowed to choose some of their own local officials. It was not until the population reached 60,000 that a territory could become a **state**.

The need for unity

With the British army gone, the Americans now had to defend themselves. In order to survive economically, they needed to trade with other parts of the world. All of this was difficult for individual states to achieve because they were too small.

The states in the South were very different from those in the North. The southern states had many cotton and tobacco plantations (estates). The northern states were made up of farmers and merchants many of whom were descended from the Puritan and Quaker settlers of the 16th century. The southern plantations depended on slave labour whereas slavery was frowned upon by many people in the North, even though they were not particularly sympathetic towards

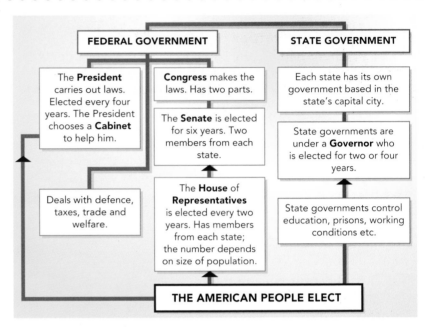

▲ The system of government in the USA.

negroes. So the new states were anxious to keep some of their newly won independence for themselves.

Federal Government

The result was a **federal** system of government. This meant that there was a central government in Washington that made important decisions on matters that affected all the states, such as defence. But each state also had a government of its own in each state capital. This made decisions about such things as law and order and education. The President of the United States was the head of state for the whole of the USA but each State Governor was also very powerful. This is still the way in which the USA is governed today.

'Government by the people, for the people'

This ideal, which we call **democracy**, was firmly established in the US constitution. As you can see from the diagram the people were involved at almost every level, in the choice of their government either directly or indirectly. Above all, the government was responsible for protecting the rights and freedom and property of the individual.

The USA's system of government was not firmly established in the East when expansion westwards began. The original states in the North and South did not get on well. They disagreed particularly over **slavery**.

On the one hand, the constitution protected the freedom of the individual. So what about the position of the slaves? On the other hand, slaves were the property of their owners. The constitution promised to protect property. The plantation owners in the South argued that they could not run their estates without slave labour and that their slaves were valuable property. By 1860 there were over three and a half million slaves in the USA.

The disputes grew worse as settlers went West. The decision had to be made whether slavery was to be allowed in the new territories. In 1850, when California became a state, it was decided that there was to be no slavery. Then, in 1860, South Carolina decided to break away from the USA. The other southern states followed and tried to set up their own form of government. The northern states wanted to keep the states united so, in 1861, the **American Civil War** began between the North and the South. It lasted until 1865 when slavery was abolished and the Union of states was firmly established. Prejudices against Negroes remained however, particularly in the South. Meanwhile, settlers were moving westwards in increasing numbers, and this migration was to have an enormous effect on the Indian way of life. It is now time to look more closely at the Plains Indians and their lives before the arrival of the white man.

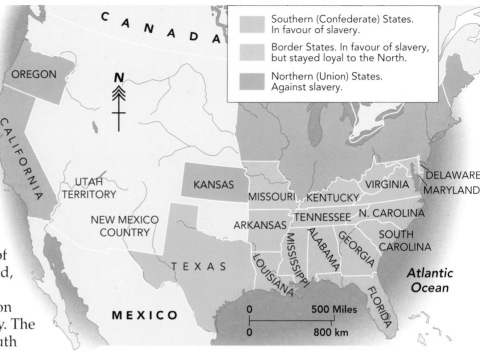

Southern (Confederate) States. In favour of slavery.

Border States. In favour of slavery, but stayed loyal to the North.

Northern (Union) States. Against slavery.

▲ The divisions between the Northern and Southern states in the Civil War 1861–5.

SUMMARY

▶ **1840** The Mississippi River was the western frontier of the thirteen East coast states – the USA as founded in 1783. Beyond lived the Plains Indians.

▶ **1843** The first settlers arrived in Oregon.

▶ **1846** The USA acquired Oregon from Britain.

▶ **1846–8** War with Mexico. The USA gained Texas and Pacific coast lands.

▶ **1846–7** The Mormons trek to the Great Salt Lake.

▶ **1848** Gold discovered in California. Gold rush.

▶ **1850s** The first homesteaders began to move on to the Plains.

▶ **1861–5** Civil war between the northern and southern states. The North won. Slavery abolished. Union established.

▶ **1866** The first 'long drive' of Texas Longhorns.

▶ **1869** A railway was completed across America.

▶ **1870s** Cattle ranching began on the Plains. The native Indians were gradually moved off.

CHAPTER 2

THE WORLD OF THE PLAINS INDIANS

The massive tract of land that lies in the heart of North America is nowadays called the Great Plains. The pioneers of the 1840s saw it as the 'Great American Desert' – a region to be crossed as quickly as possible in order to reach the more attractive lands of Oregon and California. But this 'Desert' had for centuries been the home of the Native Indians – and they saw it very differently. The map shows the distribution of the main Plains Indian tribes. They did not make up a single Indian 'nation'; they were descended from the peoples who had migrated to the American continent many centuries before. This chapter will highlight the similarities of outlook from tribe to tribe as well as the differences. It will show how most of the tribes came to rely on hunting for their livelihood – and how this led to a largely nomad culture, with carefully-defined roles for men and women, young and old. Finally it will describe how the tribes organized themselves politically and why and how they went to war. The contrast could not have been greater between the culture of the Indians and that of the white settlers who were about to launch their great drive westward. This did not make warfare between the two peoples inevitable, but in an atmosphere of mutual suspicion and intolerance, it made conflict very likely.

Source A

We did not think of the great open plains, the beautiful rolling hills, and winding streams with tangled growth , as 'wild' . . .
To us it was tame. Earth was bountiful and we were surrounded with the blessings of the Great Mystery.

▲ Luther Standing Bear, *My People the Sioux*, 1975.

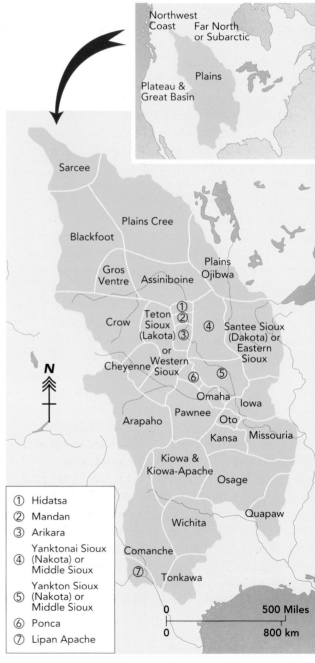

① Hidatsa
② Mandan
③ Arikara
④ Yanktonai Sioux (Nakota) or Middle Sioux
⑤ Yankton Sioux (Nakota) or Middle Sioux
⑥ Ponca
⑦ Lipan Apache

▲ The area occupied by the Plains Indians and where the different tribes were based in the 19th century.

2.1 Who were the Plains Indians?

The Indians who lived on the Great Plains had many things in common but they were not alike in every way. The Plains Indians consisted of over 30 different tribes, each was distinctive in appearance and language. Each had its own history, myths and stories which were passed down orally through every generation. They were also recognizable by the distinctive decorations on their clothing, moccasins (soft leather shoes), parfleches (large rawhide bags), saddles and tipis (tent-like homes). At the beginning of the 19th century, each had its own recognized territory on the Plains. The Blackfeet, Assiniboine and Crow tribes dominated the northern Plains. In the central Plains, the Sioux and Cheyenne were the largest tribes. In fact, the Sioux had so many tribes and sub-tribes that they were known as a 'nation'. The southern Plains were the home of the Comanche, Kiowa, Arapaho and Kiowa Apache tribes. By 1840 many of the tribes of the Plains had been reduced in size as a result of a serious outbreak of smallpox which had struck in 1836–7. The disease had been caught from white traders. The Indians had no natural resistance to white people's illnesses – a bad omen for the future.

The common bond between almost all of the tribes was that their survival depended largely on hunting. They were, therefore, mostly nomadic as they needed to follow the huge herds of buffalo that roamed the Plains. Some of the tribes that lived on the edges of the Plains in the early 1800s also grew crops. The Mandans are a good example. Whilst hunting the buffalo was very important to them, they also grew maize and squash. One of George Catlin's paintings shows them living in semi-permanent villages, in dome-shaped earth lodges (shelters) rather than the temporary Plains tipi (see Source D on page 20). The Pawnee and Osage tribes lived in a similar way to the Mandans, trading their own produce for the dried buffalo meat and skins of the hunting tribes.

▲ A Blackfoot Indian

▶ A Dakota Sioux

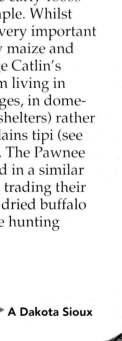

▲ Assiniboine with horned headdress

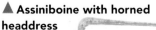

Life for the Plains Indians was hard. Their attitudes, beliefs and way of living were deeply affected by this struggle to survive. It is important to recognize this in order to understand the culture of the Indians.

Why was the buffalo so important?

When the tribes first settled on the Plains, many of them grew crops as well as hunting the buffalo that lived there in huge herds. By the 19th century, survival for most of the tribes on the Plains depended on their success in hunting the buffalo. They were able to use almost every part of the animal to provide them with what they needed for daily living (see diagram).

This dependence on the buffalo determined how the hunter-Indians lived. The buffalo roamed. This meant that the Indians were obliged to follow the herds wherever they went on the Plains. So these tribes were **nomadic** and they abandoned farming. Their nomadic existence influenced the style of their homes, their family and community life, their ideas of bravery, their tribal organization and their laws and punishments. In other words, the life of the Indians was completely bound up with the buffalo – so much so, that the destruction of the buffalo would inevitably mean the destruction of the culture of the Indians.

The homes and villages of the majority of the tribes of the Plains had to be temporary. The tribes themselves were subdivided many times into smaller groups or **bands**, made up of several families. This ensured that at any one time, large numbers of Indians were not killing buffalo from the same herd. The Indians were very conscious of the need to conserve the buffalo. So the whole tribe met only in the summer in a huge tribal gathering.

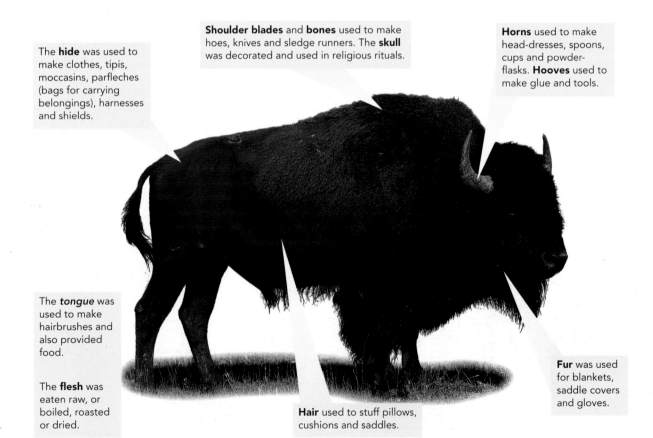

The **hide** was used to make clothes, tipis, moccasins, parfleches (bags for carrying belongings), harnesses and shields.

Shoulder blades and **bones** used to make hoes, knives and sledge runners. The **skull** was decorated and used in religious rituals.

Horns used to make head-dresses, spoons, cups and powder-flasks. **Hooves** used to make glue and tools.

The *tongue* was used to make hairbrushes and also provided food.

The **flesh** was eaten raw, or boiled, roasted or dried.

Hair used to stuff pillows, cushions and saddles.

Fur was used for blankets, saddle covers and gloves.

How did the Indians find the Buffalo?

In order to follow the buffalo, the tribes needed to be able to find them. The Indians could live without hunting for as long as their supplies of dried buffalo meat lasted. Once these supplies were used up, they had to be replaced. So a buffalo herd had to be found. Sometimes this was done by young braves, but the tribes also tried to make contact with the buffalo using the spirit world through their dances. George Catlin, who travelled and lived among the Indians of the Plains, wrote a description of a buffalo dance performed by some of the Mandan tribe (Source B).

Once the herd had been located, the village was moved. This had to be done quickly and was usually supervised by a special group of braves. The Cheyennes called this special group **Dog Soldiers**. Among other duties they took care of the whole village on the move, chose camp sites and ensured that the buffalo herds were not frightened away. The Dog Soldiers also made sure that only the right number of animals was slaughtered on the hunt so that the buffalo would never become extinct.

Source B

The chief issues his order to his runners who proclaim through the village – and in a few minutes the dance begins. About ten or fifteen Mandans at a time join in the dance, each one with the skin of the buffalo's head (or mask) with horns on, placed over his head, and in his hand his favourite bow or lance, with which he is used to slay the buffalo.

This dance never fails, nor can it, for it cannot be stopped [but is going incessantly day and night] until 'buffalo come'. Drums are beating and rattles are shaken, and songs and yells are shouted, and onlookers stand ready with masks on their heads, and weapons in hand, to take the place of each one as he becomes fatigued.

During this time 'lookers' are kept on the hills in the neighbourhood of the village. When they discover buffaloes in sight they give the signal, by 'throwing their robes'. At this joyful intelligence, there is a shout of thanks to the Great Spirit! These dances have sometimes been continued in this village two and three weeks without stopping.

▲ A description of a Mandan buffalo dance as observed by George Catlin.

Source A

◀ Painting by George Catlin of a Mandan buffalo dance (1833). Notice the dome-shaped lodges of the Mandans. Unlike many other tribes of the Plains, the Mandan lived in semi-permanent villages.

The buffalo hunt

Young Indian braves gained honour and respect in the tribe by showing their skill and bravery in the hunt. Consequently, there was much more at stake on a hunting expedition than successfully killing the buffalo or 'bison'.

Until the 16th century, the Indians needed speed, skill and accuracy because the buffalo were hunted on foot. They had to get near to the animal in order to kill it with their short bows (about one metre in length) and arrows. However, when the Spanish arrived in America in the 16th century, they brought horses with them. The arrival of the horse transformed the hunt. Indian braves became swift and skilful riders. The Comanche and Blackfeet were particularly adept on horseback. Nevertheless, confronting the buffalo also required a great deal of courage. These huge animals were killed at close range and the hunt must often have ended in tragedy (see Source C). It is not surprising that young braves gained so much esteem as they risked their lives to ensure the survival of the band or tribe.

The importance of horses

Horses made a great difference to the lives of the Indians. At first they obtained horses through trade. Then some tribes bred their own, often trading them for guns and amunition. They soon became highly prized. This can be seen in the elaborate decorations which some tribes, like the Crow, put on their horse equipment. The Shishoni hung their most precious possessions around the necks of their horses.

Source C

Source D

One morning the crier came around the village calling out that we were going to break camp . . . Then the crier said, 'Many bison, I have heard! Your children, you must take care of them!' He meant to keep the children close while travelling, so that they would not scare the bison.

After we had been travelling a while, we came to a place where there were many turnips growing, and the crier said, 'Take off your loads and let your horses rest. Take your sticks and dig turnips for yourselves.'

When the sun was high, the advisers found a place to camp. Then the crier shouted, 'Your horses make ready! We shall go forth with arrows. Plenty of meat we shall make!'

Then the head man went around picking out the best hunters with the fastest horses, and to these he said, 'Young warriors, your work I know is good; so today you will feed the helpless. You shall help the old and the young and whatever you kill shall be theirs.' This was a great honour for young men.

▲ Black Elk, holy man of the Oglala Sioux, remembers the preparation for a bison hunt. He was born in 1863.

◄ *The Buffalo Hunt* painted by Frederick Remington in 1890, after he had spent some time in Montana and the Big Horn Mountains.

The Comanche called the horse a 'god dog' and the Sioux their 'medicine dog'. So Indians would go to war to capture horses. The theft of horses from an enemy was seen as an act of bravery and the possession of horses was a symbol of wealth.

On the other hand, it has been suggested by historians that, in the long term, the arrival of the horse was probably disastrous. They argue that Indians were more careless about the number of buffalo that they slaughtered. More importantly, the ease of finding and killing the buffalo meant that many tribes, between the 17th and 19th centuries, gave up growing crops as an additional source of food and so lost the skills of planting and growing. So, when the buffalo did not appear, tribes could literally starve to death.

Women and the hunt

While the men were hunting, the women made preparations back in the newly-established camp. They prepared the fires for the feast to celebrate the hunt, and collected branches and sticks to make frames. The red meat was hung on these frames to dry so that there would be supplies of meat for some time. Later, they had the task of pegging out the skins of the buffalo. This kept the skin stretched while it dried. The women used sharp bone scrapers to remove any pieces of meat that had been left on the skin. After the skins had dried, it was the women who made them into clothing, equipment or tipi covers and decorated them beautifully, often using porcupine quills and coloured dyes.

Decoration was highly skilled work which took months to complete. Indian women formed themselves into societies based on their skills and these societies gave them some status in the tribe. Women of the Cheyenne, for example, who became highly skilled in these arts, formed the **Quiller Society** and anyone wanting to be admitted had to be initiated into the group. Women of the Arapaho produced striking designs and patterns in beadwork.

▲ Painting of a Cree woman by Karl Bodmer (1833). Her deerskin dress is a typical Plains style as are her shell and bead ear-rings. The tattoos on her chin were more common among the Cree tribe than other tribes.

QUESTIONS

1 In what ways did the buffalo hunt enable young men to show their skill and courage?

2 'Hunting the buffalo involved the whole family'. How does the information on this page and Source D support this claim?

3 Look carefully at Source C. What is Remington showing in this painting?

Nomadic Indians lived in **tipis**. These were made by the women who sewed together a huge semi-circular cover of buffalo hides. This was placed over a number of wooden poles erected in the shape of a cone to withstand the strong winds of the Plains. Flaps at the top could be moved to draw up the smoke from the fire and pipes inside, depending on the direction of the wind. Finally the buffalo hide cover was decorated. The Crows usually left their tipis unpainted but the Lakota decorated theirs with geometric patterns, and the Blackfeet with brightly coloured paintings of important animals and birds. Some ceremonial tipis were huge. Inside, they were made comfortable with rugs and cushions.

The tipis could be taken down at a moment's notice if the band had to move off to follow the buffalo. Again this was the job of the women. The tipi poles, hide cover and all the family's possessions could easily be packed on to a kind of sledge called a **travois** (see Source B). This had long poles and was light enough to be pulled either by hand or to be harnessed to a dog or horse.

On these journeys, women carried their babies in **cradle-boards**. These were often very beautifully decorated. Babies were encouraged from an early age not to cry for a noisy baby

Source A

▲ This painting shows typical Indian tipis. Usually the tipis would be more widely spaced, probably in a circle.

Source B

◀ A painting by Charles Russell called *Indian Women Moving Camp* (1898). The arrival of the horse helped women in their work; notice the travois behind.

could cause a herd of grazing buffalo to stampede or warn enemies if they were nearby.

Within each nomadic tribe and band, most families were related to each other. Each member had a vital role to play. The men hunted and fought. The women provided home, food and clothing. In tribes like the Mandan and Pawnee they also had responsibility for crops, searched for edible roots and plants, and dug up wild turnips. Children were prepared for their future roles as braves and squaws (wives) by being made to work hard too.

The boys were taught to ride and to use their bows and arrows. They went on their first hunt at the age of fourteen. Children also acted as unofficial look-outs. Playing on the outskirts of the village they could give warning of unwelcome visitors. Above all, they had to be tough and to survive the harsh climate of the Plains. A traveller in

Source C

Both he and his squaw, like most other Indians, were very fond of their children, whom they never punished except in extreme cases, when they threw a bowl of cold water over them.

▲ Written by Francis Parkman in 1840. Parkman (1823–93) was an historian, traveller and writer who lived among the Indians during the 1840s.

▶ A picture of an Indian family entitled 'Days of Long Ago' painted by Henry Farny in 1903. By this time, the traditional lifestyle of the Indians had been totally destroyed.

Source D

When we were about to start on our way from the village, my attention was directed to a very aged and emaciated [thin] man, who . . . was to be left to starve.
His friends and his children were preparing in a little time to be on the march. He told them to leave him. 'I am old', he said, 'and too feeble to march. My children our nation is poor, and it is necessary that you should all go to the country where you can get meat. My strength is no more, my days are nearly numbered, and I am a burden to my children. I cannot go and I wish to die.'

▲ George Catlin, *Manners, Customs and Condition of the North American Indians*, 1844. Catlin (1796–1872) spent a lot of time among the Indians in the 1830s.

Source E

In 1846, being seventeen years of age, I was admitted to the council of warriors . . . Perhaps the greatest joy to me was that now I could marry the fair Alope . . . She was a slender, delicate girl and we had loved each other for a long time. So, I went to see her father . . . .he asked many ponies for her. I made no reply but in a few days appeared before his wigwam [tipi] with the herd of ponies and took with me Alope. This was all the marriage ceremony necessary in our tribe.

▲ **Geronimo, an Apache chief, describes his marriage.**

Source G

The son of this chief, a youth of eighteen years distinguished himself by taking four wives in one day! I visited the wigwam [tipi] of this young man several times, and saw his four little wives seated round the fire, where all were entering very happily on the duties of married life . . . In this country polygamy is allowed, for where there are two or three times the number of women than there are men, such an arrangement answers a good purpose, for the females are taken care of.

▲ **George Catlin commenting on a polygamous marriage.**

QUESTIONS

1 Read Sources D and G Does Catlin approve or disapprove of the Indians in these sources?

2 Look at Source E. What impression of Indian life is Henry Farny trying to give? Is this accurate?

3 In what ways did village and family life reflect the Indians' struggle to survive on the Plains?

1821 was amazed to see a group of Indian children playing, naked, in freezing water! Children were corrected but were never physically punished. Parents celebrated the success of a son's first hunt and proudly announced a daughter's first menstrual period as a recognition of her womanhood.

The elderly also played their part in village life. Old men were sometimes 'story-tellers' who passed on the history of the tribe, so that the children would have pride in the achievements of their ancestors. But once the old people became helpless they were left to die.

What attitude did the Indians have to marriage?

When young braves were in a position to be able to support a wife, they wooed the girl of their choice with poetry and music made on the beautifully carved flutes that they had made. In most tribes, marriages were usually love-matches, so if the girl was sufficiently impressed by the bravery of her suitor and his efforts to win her, she would eventually accept his proposal. Girls were told by their grandmothers and mothers never to accept the first request. Their fathers had also to be impressed by what the young man had to offer him. This was usually horses. When the couple became engaged, they exchanged rings, and the engagement could last for five or six years.

Arranged marriages were usual in some tribes, for example, the Cheyenne. But, in other tribes, they took place when a woman was left with no one to take care of her. Because there were fewer men than women, Indians practised **polygamy** (having more than one wife). This ensured that no woman was left without support. Widows, particularly, benefited from this.

Women owned quite a lot of property including the tipi that she made, the family possessions, such as hides and the children when they were born. Her new husband would move into the tipi of her family. So, although the man was the head of the household, his wife also had some prestige. Women who were particularly skilful earned great respect – for example, members of the Quiller Society. The man could set aside or divorce his wife by a simple announcement. But, if his wife owned the tipi and all the family belongings, he could find himself with nothing. So divorce was quite rare.

Source A

I have heard it said by some very good men, and some who have been preaching the Christian religion amongst them, that Indians have no religion but only ignorant superstition. I assert that the North American Indian is everywhere, in his native state, a highly moral and religious being.

◀ George Catlin, *Manners, Customs and Condition of the North American Indians*, 1844.

Source B

Young men go up on to a hill, and cry and pray for some animal or bird to come to them. For five or six days they neither eat nor drink, and they become very thin. While in this state they dream, and whatever animal or bird they see in their dreams becomes their medicine and guardian through life.

▲ J.G. Frazer, *The Native Races of America*, 1939.

▼ A robe decorated with the circle design which had great religious significance.

Nature's great circle

The Plains Indian tribes all shared a sense of unity with nature. They saw themselves as part of nature. They admired the qualities of many animals and believed that they shared the land with all other living things so no one could own it. The natural world produced them all and they would return to the earth. So the circle had special significance for them. It described the cycle of life from birth until death and also the seasons of the year, from the spring until the onset of winter. The world was round and their villages and tipis (tent-like homes) were round. The circle appears on many of the designs on tipis and clothing.

These beliefs may have developed because, like the animals that lived on the Plains, the Indians were driven by the need to survive. Most importantly, it gave them a great respect and love for the whole of nature – plants, birds and animals. They did not feel superior to these in any way. In fact, many of these creatures appeared among the decorations on Indian tipis and had great religious importance.

What was Indian 'medicine'?

Almost all the Indian tribes believed in a supreme being or god known as the Great Spirit. He had created the whole of nature and was all powerful. This belief explains the Indians' total respect for all living things because, like themselves, they were all the creation of the Great Spirit.

The world of all of the Indians was full of spirits. Every animal, tree and plant had its own spirit which the Indians had to have on their side. So they undertook complicated and painful ceremonies in order to call on the spirits to be with them.

Source C

The spirits were what they called their 'medicine'. Young braves believed they could discover the animals and plants that were their own particular 'medicine', as part of their path to manhood. They did this by fasting, then praying and waiting for an animal or bird to appear to them in a vision. Whatever creature appeared would then be their guardian spirit. They killed the animal and made it into a 'medicine bag'. Other objects were put into this bag which was worn by the brave. Only he knew what the bag contained and he would not be parted from it.

'Medicine men'

Indians depended on the medicine man to interpret their visions and to make contact with the spirit world. These were men who had special powers. They were usually men with strong personalities and unusual wisdom. Sometimes, they associated themselves with an animal by wearing its skin in their rituals (ceremonies). They claimed that this animal gave them their powers. The bear was a favourite.

Medicine men were also called upon to cure the sick and to use their wisdom to advise the elders and chiefs when they were in meetings of the council. All Indians believed that through their contact with the spirit world they derived from the medicine men all the power that they needed to perform these tasks. But they also believed that there was power in the animal world.

Animal power

Certain animals were especially powerful. For example, a brave could discover if he would die young or old by looking at his reflection in a pool of the blood of a dead badger. The Sioux, Crow and Assiniboine tribes regarded the bull elk as being strong 'medicine' in the pursuit of the women they loved. So they used its bones to make the very beautiful flutes that they played to serenade them. These were called 'elk whistles'. The Comanches looked out for a horned toad when they were searching for the buffalo because they believed that it would show them the way to the herds. The Blackfeet had beaver medicine bundles. These were beaver skins full of the skins and bones of animals. These were sometimes opened up and songs and chants were performed to call the spirits of the game that they needed for food. These medicine bundles were highly prized.

▼ Medicine man of the Hidatsa tribe in the costume of the Dog Dance, painted by Karl Bodmer, in about 1834.

Source E

The medicine men would lift the young man and lay him under the pole. An old man would then come forward with a very sharp pointed knife. He would take hold of the breast of the young brave, pull the skin forward and pierce it through with the knife. Then he would insert a wooden pin . . . through the slit and tie a strong buckskin thong to this pin.

From the pole two rawhide ropes were suspended. The candidate would now be lifted up . . . and was hanging from his breast . . . Although the blood would be running down from the knife incision, the candidate would smile, although everyone knew he must be suffering intense pain.

▲ Description of a Sun Dance from *My Family the Sioux*, by Luther Standing Bear. Amongst the Sioux, young men sometimes offered themselves for the Sun Dance when someone in the family was ill. The young man described here by Luther Standing Bear had chosen to offer himself for this purpose.

How did the Indians contact the spirits?

There were times when all of the Indians in a band or tribe needed to make contact themselves with the spirits. They did this by performing dance rituals. Women were involved in many of these rituals. For example, the Cheyenne and Comanche performed the massaum or animal dance. During this ceremony, the women carried a sacred buffalo skull into a special lodge as part of the efforts of the band to get the spirits to bless them with plenty of buffalo. Other tribes such as the Mandan carried out Buffalo dances to summon the buffalo in times of need (see page 18).

Dances were an important part of religious life. There were dances associated with going to war and the **Scalp Dance** was performed to celebrate any victories. The most common dance amongst all tribes was the **Sun Dance**. This was more of a ritual than a dance. It challenged young braves to show their courage by exposing themselves to torture and pain. They were hauled from the ground, facing the sun, by straps attached to wooden skewers which were passed through the flesh on their chests. This caused excruciating pain during which time the Indians believed that the spirit was freed and worldly things were left behind. In some tribes, they endured further pain by allowing their fingers and toes to be cut off. The medicine man presided over this 'dance'. It ended when he decided that the ritual was complete. Not all Indians, however, tortured themselves as part of the Sun Dance ritual. The Cree and Assiniboine used this ceremony for prayer and contemplation.

SUMMARY

▶ Indians believed in the great circle of nature.

▶ All Indians believed in powerful spirits which gave helpful medicine or charms.

▶ Medicine men were especially gifted at channelling the powers of the spirit world.

▶ The power of animals was believed to be very important.

▶ Dances were an essential part of religious rituals.

QUESTIONS

1 How do the beliefs of the Indians show their closeness to nature?

2 What further evidence do you have in this section of the role of women in the tribe?

3 Why did animals play such an important part in the religious beliefs of Indians?

In Chapter 1 you read about the Constitution of the USA. This document laid down how people should be elected to govern the country, how laws should be made and kept, and what rights all people should have. The Indians, a people who were always on the move and struggling to survive, had no such constitution. Nor did they live by the laws of the USA. But this does not mean that the tribes lacked order or organization.

How powerful were the chiefs?

At the tribal Council, the chiefs sat in a huge circle. They smoked the ceremonial pipe to bring wisdom to their discussions and continued to talk until decisions about war and peace had been made. Usually, they talked until everyone agreed to accept the decisions of the Council. But it seems that loyalty to a tribe was not always as strong as loyalty to the band within it. The chiefs had no power of their own to force their will on the people. So a sub-tribe or band could do as it pleased.

Soldier societies

Within the band, the chief and Council of Elders were usually helped by the soldier societies. Every man in the band could belong to one of these societies, as long as he had distinguished himself in some way. In some tribes these were very select. For example, the Kiowa tribe had a society called the

▲ The Chief of the Mandan tribe.

Source A

The chief has no control over the limbs, or liberty of his subjects, nor no other power whatever, excepting that of **influence**. [This] he gains by his virtues and his exploits in war. In fact, he is no more than a **leader** whom every young warrior may follow, or . . . go back from . . . if he is willing to meet the disgrace that awaits him who deserts his chief in the hour of danger.

▲ George Catlin decribing the government of the Indians.

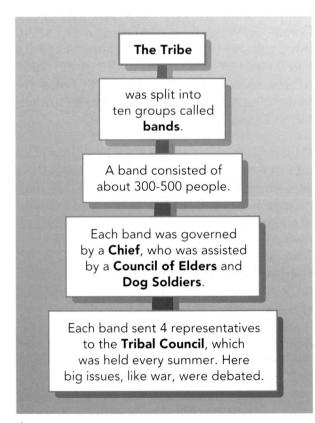

The Tribe

was split into ten groups called **bands**.

A band consisted of about 300-500 people.

Each band was governed by a **Chief**, who was assisted by a **Council of Elders** and **Dog Soldiers**.

Each band sent 4 representatives to the **Tribal Council**, which was held every summer. Here big issues, like war, were debated.

▲ How the Cheyenne tribe was governed

Kaitsenko (the ten bravest) which always led attacks on the enemy. In the Cheyenne tribe there were six societies – the Fox Soldiers, Crazy Dogs, Elk Soldiers, Red Shields, Bowstrings and Dog Soldiers (see page 17).

Indian punishments

Indians did not have 'laws' as we know them. They were expected to behave in a certain way according to custom. So a brave could be humiliated in public for being boastful about his achievements in hunting or warfare. His pride would be greatly injured which was far worse to an Indian brave than being physically punished. The tribes differed in their treatment of more serious crimes. In some, a man who committed murder was made to look after the family of his victim. The Cheyenne expelled murderers from the band. It was not considered to be a crime to steal horses from an enemy.

Tribal warfare

It has been commonly believed that Indians went to war to protect their hunting grounds or to obtain horses. It also helped the elders of the band to control the younger braves who wanted to win honour and respect. Peter Farb, an American historian, has suggested that there is a more important reason. He says that survival depended on the tribes remaining unified. This was difficult to achieve because they lived in bands, which went their own way most of the time. Warfare was very effective in bringing the tribe together to face a common enemy. By 1840 many of the tribes in the West, such as the Comanches and the Apaches were traditional enemies.

What did warfare mean to Indians?

The main objective in warfare was not necessarily to kill the enemy, even though the Indians fought with bows, arrows, tomahawks and, later, guns. They killed if they had to, but the real honour came from **counting coup**. This meant getting close enough to the enemy, while he was alive, to touch him with a specially decorated coup stick. Similar skill and courage was needed

Source B

War has been transformed into a great game in which scoring against the enemy often takes precedence over killing him. The scoring is in the counting of coup – touching or striking an enemy with hand or weapons . . . . A man's rank as a warrior depends on two factors: his total 'score' in coups, and his ability to lead successful raids in which Cheyenne losses are low. Actual killing and scalping get their credit, too, but they do not rate as highly as the show-off deeds.

▲ **From a book about the Cheyennes written in 1978.**

Source C

The Indian concept of bravery was completely different from that of the European settlers. The Comanche thought it stupid to stand and fight when there was no chance of winning anything save honour; instead they would slink away from such a contest, to return another day to steal horses, booty and captives.

▲ **Odie B. Faulk** *The Crimson Desert.*

to hunt buffalo successfully. The successes of a brave were recorded by the feathers that he wore on his head. These brought him great respect in the band, as did the number of horses that he managed to capture.

Counting coup was seen by white people as evidence that the Indians regarded war as a game. Certainly, the Indians had no intention of being killed themselves. If death threatened, they quickly retreated. White people saw this, and the custom of 'creeping up' on the enemy as cowardice. For white people, courage meant facing the enemy, and death in battle was an honour. But the Indians believed that a dead brave was of little use to his family and the band – so there was no honour in death for them.

Why did Indians scalp their enemies?

Indians took scalps as trophies of their achievements in battle and displayed them outside their tipis. But when an Indian took the scalp of his enemy he also took his spirit so that he could not go to the afterlife. In this way, the Indian made sure that he would not meet his enemies when he got there himself. Sometimes, a man survived scalping but still believed he had lost his spirit. He could only get this back by taking the scalp of another enemy.

Wherever the white settlers moved, the Indians' way of life was disrupted. This was seen particularly dramatically on the Plains, where the Indians were displaced by gold prospectors, cattle ranchers and homesteaders who condemned the Indians as 'savage' and 'uncivilized'. From 1840 it was harder and harder for them to resist the westward-bound white settlers.

2.6 EXERCISE

1 Explain in detail why each of the following was so important to the Indians:
  a The circle
  b The buffalo
  c The land and the natural world
  d The Great Spirit
  e Medicine men
  f Dog Soldiers and the soldier societies
  g Scalping

2 If Indians had respect for all living things, why did they go to war?

3 Read this Cheyenne proverb.
'A nation is not conquered until the hearts of its women are on the ground. Then it is done, no matter how brave its warriors nor how strong their weapons.'

  a What does this proverb (saying) tell you about the attitude of the Cheyenne towards their women?
  b Use the information in this chapter to explain why the women of the Plains Indians were thought to be so important.

4 Study the following two views of the Indians.

View A
From what I have seen of these people I say that there is nothing very strange in their character. It is a simple one, and easy to be understood if the right means be taken to familiarize ourselves with it. The Native American Indian in his native state is an honest, faithful, brave, warlike, cruel, revengeful, relentless – yet honourable, contemplative and religious being.
Written by George Catlin in 1841.

View B
The Indians are children. Their wars, their treaties, habitations, crafts, comforts, all being to the very lowest ages of human existence. Squalid and conceited, proud and worthless, lazy and lousy, they will strut out or drink out their miserable existence, and at length afford the world relief by dying out of it.
Written by Horace Greeley. He was the editor of a newspaper and believed in 'manifest destiny'. He wrote this as a result of a journey across the USA in 1859.

  a What knowledge and evidence about the Indians will Catlin have used to reach his conclusion?
  b On what evidence has Greeley based his view of the Indians?
  c Why is Catlin's view of the Indians different from that of Horace Greeley?
  d What might Greeley's motives have been when he wrote this?
  e Which of the two sources do you consider to be the more reliable? Explain your answer carefully.

CHAPTER 3

TRAILBLAZERS

'It is on the stroke of seven; the rushing to and fro, the cracking of whips, the loud command to oxen and what seems to be the unavoidable confusion of the last ten minutes has ceased . . . The clear notes of the trumpet sound in the front; the pilot and his guards mount their horses, the leading division of the wagons moves out of the encampment and takes up the line of march, the rest fall into their places with the precision of clockwork. . . .' And so began a typical day on the great trek West across America. Jesse Applegate was there in 1843 to describe the leaving of yet another overnight camp of a wagon train on the trail.

In this chapter you will read about the people who blazed the first trails (routes) into the American unknown; the mountain men, the animal-trappers, the farmers, the gold-diggers and Mormons. Some were greedy, some were desperate, all in their own ways were brave. But for whatever reasons they left the East, thousands more were going to follow in their wagon tracks in one of history's most fascinating migrations.

Jim Bridger: profile of a mountain man

Bridger was born in 1804 in Richmond, Virginia. In 1822 he was attracted by an advertisement for fur trappers. In 1824, on a beaver-hunting expedition, he discovered the Great Salt Lake. He was a man of independent spirit who loved to roam the mountains and plains. In 1830 he bought the Rocky Mountain Fur Company with four others but the fur trade declined so, in 1843, he built Fort Bridger on the Oregon Trail. Here he provided a store, a workshop and a forge to look after the needs of travellers. Although he bought a farm in the 1850s, he continued to work as a guide. During his life in the West, he travelled through Idaho, Wyoming, Montana, Utah and North and South Dakota. He could not read or write but he spoke French and ten Indian languages.

He was accepted by the Indians and understood their ways, possibly because he had three Indian wives in succession. In the 1870s he went blind and in 1881 died on his farm near Kansas City. This is how he was described by an acquaintance: 'Straight as an Indian . . . there was nothing in his deportment to indicate the heroic spirit that dwelled within, simply a plain, unassuming man.'

3.1 Who were the first trailblazers?

Mountain men and trappers were men who made a living by trapping animals – mainly beavers – and selling their skins back in the East. They were wild solitary figures, who lived like the Native Indians with whom they traded. Several married Indian women. One, **Jim Beckworth**, actually became an Indian chief. Another, **Jeremiah Johnson**, became a legendary figure because of his personal crusade against the Indians who had killed and scalped his pregnant wife in 1847.

These mountain men were also adventurers and explorers. They knew the Sierra Nevada, the Rockies, the Plateaux, the Plains and the Pacific coastland in great detail. They told of their experiences when they returned to the East. Sometimes their stories appeared in newspapers or magazines. It was these stories that inspired many people to migrate westwards. The descriptions in the stories also helped early travellers to plan their routes. **Joseph Walker** helped to pioneer the Santa Fe Trail and **Jedediah Smith** planned the route through the Rockies (the South Pass) to Oregon and California. **Jim Bridger** and others became guides to wagon trains. These were the great pathfinders.

John Charles Frémont was also an adventurer and pathfinder. He had Government support to undertake his own expeditions which were based on information from the mountain men. In 1842 he carried out a survey of the Rocky Mountains using Jedediah Smith's route through the South Pass. Between 1843 and 1844, with the help of the US Army Corps of Topographical Engineers, he surveyed and mapped out the Oregon Trail. The US Government ordered 10,000 copies of the report and map to be printed, illustrating the importance it attached to the idea of manifest destiny! (See page 11) Frémont's report, and the images of the West that it created, were highly influential in encouraging further migration.

What was the great migration?

In 1843, a year before Frémont's map was published, the first group of settlers left Independence, Missouri to begin what became known as the **great migration**. All told, about 1,000 men, women and children travelled the 3,200 kilometres to Oregon, which at that time was owned jointly by Britain and the USA.

▼ **The trails to the Pacific coastlands.**

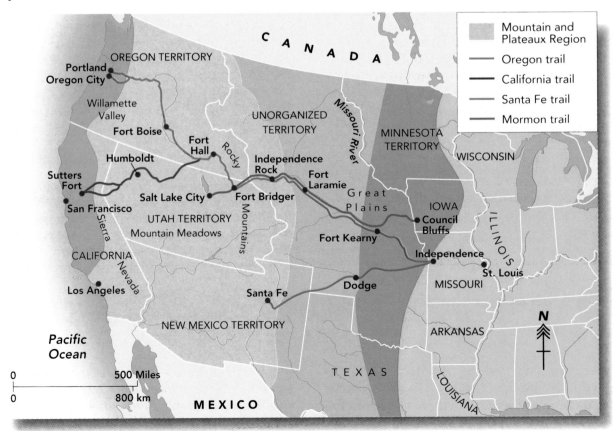

Each family had its own covered wagon. They joined together with many other families to form a wagon train for safety and guidance along the trail.

At Independence these hardy families were fitted out with wagons and horses. Supplies for the journey were taken on, although the first people who set off did not know what would be needed or how much could be carried. The covered wagons were also loaded with the family's most treasured possessions. Few of these precious items ever reached Oregon! They had to be left by the wayside to lighten the wagons before dangerous rivers could be crossed or mountain passes climbed.

▲ *Emigrants Crossing the Plains*, painted by Albert Bierstadt in 1867. He was a German-born artist who was fascinated by the natural beauty of the West. His paintings were very popular with people who still lived in the East in the 1860s.

The wagon train crossed the Plains along the Platte River and rested at Fort Laramie before crossing the Rockies through the South Pass. This was 1,600 kilometres from Independence and 2,280 metres up in the Rocky Mountains. After a stop for repairs and provisions at Fort Bridger, the journey continued across the Plateaux region. This was one of the most difficult sections of the trail since it involved crossing the tributaries of the Green River before reaching Fort Hall on the Snake River. Here the trail to California forked off to the south.

Where did the first migrants head for?
Oregon-bound travellers followed the Snake River to Fort Boise, and crossed the Sierra Nevada to the Columbia River where they descended into the Willamette valley of Oregon. There they could farm as they had back in the East. In the years that followed the first wagon train, thousands travelled on the Oregon Trail. By 1845 there were 6,000 Americans in Oregon, which added weight to the US Government's attempts to acquire the territory from Britain.

At first travellers to California had followed the old and difficult Santa Fe Trail. After the discovery of gold in 1848, (see page 32) a new trail was blazed from Fort Hall to Sutter's Fort (Sacramento). Until California was handed over to the USA by Mexico in 1848, there were fewer migrants to California than to Oregon.

Life on the trail
Wagon trains were strictly disciplined and usually well organized. They were led by a pilot and his scout who made the important decisions about routes, resting times and overnight camps. Wagon trains had to move at a steady pace because timing was important if they were to avoid the danger of being trapped in the mountains by snow. The journey from Independence began in the Spring. Wagons were usually so full of belongings that the people had to walk. This was only one of the many hardships that had to be endured. There were many other difficulties.

Shortages of food and water were common. Disease, especially outbreaks of cholera from polluted water, was always a threat. Stampeding animals, such as buffalo, were a danger, as were the frequent prairie fires. River-crossings were hazardous, either because of the current or the deep holes in the river bed. There were often accidents, particularly involving children.

All the trails passed through land occupied by Indians. The Government sent out army units to help and protect travellers. But in fact, many of the Indian tribes traded with the migrants. It was only when the number of migrants grew that there was serious trouble with the Indians, as we shall see in Chapter 8.

There were compensations for these hardships. Artists of the West such as **Albert Bierstadt** (see Source A on page 31) have painted its magnificent scenery. It is also claimed by some American historians that 98% of American settlers in the 1850s were literate as a result of mothers teaching their children to read when there was little else to do on the trail! Then there were the forts along the way that provided supplies as well as an opportunity to rest. Huge herds of buffalo on the Plains provided fresh meat and their dung was used for fuel.

Did the migrants see themselves as trailblazers?

Some of the migrants undoubtedly believed that their journey was very special. High up on the South Pass in the Rocky Mountains is a huge stone called **Independence Rock**. On it are carved the names of many of those who passed that way on the Oregon Trail. So many were anxious to leave a record of their achievement that a stonemason was stationed there ready to carve their names. Perhaps those on the wagon trains also recognized themselves as the trailblazers, helping to fulfil the nation's destiny.

3.2 All that glisters – is it gold?

In January 1848 James Marshall, a carpenter, was building a mill for John Sutter, of Sutter's Fort in the foothills of the Sierra Nevada. When he went to inspect the channel that had been dug for the wheel, he saw something gleaming that looked like gold. The next day Sutter confirmed that he had indeed discovered gold. At first it was kept secret, but not for long. When the news leaked out that gold had been discovered it sparked off one of the biggest mass migrations in the history of the West.

Who were the forty-niners?

By the end of 1848, 10,000 men were digging for gold in California. By 1849 there were 90,000. These new settlers came not just from other parts of America but also from countries abroad. They went to California hoping to make a fortune either by digging for gold themselves or starting up businesses there. The diggers became known as the **forty-niners**. They travelled there by sea, around Cape Horn or overland, either via the Isthmus of Panama or the Santa Fe and California Trails. The excitement that drove them there is clearly evident in Source A.

Source A

I looked for a moment; frenzy seized my soul; unbidden my legs performed entirely new movements of polka steps – I took several. Houses were too small for me to stay in . . . piles of gold rose up before me at every step, castles of marble, dazzling the eye with their rich appliances . . . in short, I had a very violent attack of gold fever.

▲ A San Francisco man writing about his reaction to hearing the news that gold had been discovered in California in 1848.

Source B

The hardships of the overland route to California are unimaginable. Care and suspense, pained anxiety, fear of losing animals and fear of being left in the mountains to starve and freeze to death, and a thousand things which no one thinks of until on the way, are things of which I may write and you may read, but are nothing to the reality.

▲ John Lloyd Stephens, a traveller and author, writing in 1849.

Source C

Suffice it to say that I know of no country in which there is so much corruption, villainy, outlawry . . . and every variety of crime, folly and meanness.

▲ From Hinton R. Helper, *The Land of Gold: Reality Versus Fiction.* **Helper went from North Carolina to California in the late 1840s, and later wrote about his experinces of the gold rush.**

Source D

The stories that you hear frequently in the States are the most extravagant lies imaginable – the mines are a humbug. All hopes of making a fortune in California are lost sight of in 99 cases out of a 100, and the almost universal feeling is to get home. It is truly heart-rending to witness the general despondency which exists among miners, and to see stout-hearted and brave men shed tears at their hopeless condition.

▲ **From a letter written by a gold prospector to his brother in 1849.**

Such enthusiasm was needed because the journey to California was in itself hazardous. Once there, life was difficult and uncomfortable.

Did everyone make a fortune?

The dreams of untold wealth were quickly shattered for most prospectors. Only a few individuals were lucky. Thousands laboured in vain because the sources of gold were limited. The mining towns themselves were wild and lawless, and living conditions were poor. This was partly because most gold diggers were under thirty years of age. They came to look for gold with the intention of returning home when they had 'struck it rich'. A gold digger finding small quantities might earn an average of $20 a day but it cost him $18 to live. Often he was left without money to return home, so life became desperate.

Their failure can be partly explained by the difficulty of extracting gold using the panning process (see Source E). There were also a large number of prospectors trying to find a very small amount of gold in the riverbeds. Those who struck significant quantities of gold found it underground. Extracting it cost large sums of money, so it was usually mined by companies from the cities in the East. They employed miners who worked in dangerous and unhealthy conditions for very little money.

Source E

▶ **Panning for gold in 1849. This was the simplest method of looking for gold. Dirt was gathered in water from the river bed. The lighter dirt was shaken away showing up the gold – if there was any there.**

What were the costs of the discovery?

The discovery of gold in 1848 had far reaching effects, both good and bad, for California and the USA as a whole. Gold attracted people from all over America as well as other parts of the world. They included Mexicans, Chinese, Indians and Negroes. Some white Americans soon considered themselves to be superior which gave rise to racial conflict. This was at a time, remember, when slavery still existed in some American states (see Chapter 1). Taxes were imposed on foreign miners and, in the mines, American workers often refused to work with the Chinese because they were thought to be inferior. The greatest sufferers were probably the native Indians of California who were virtually wiped out as a result of the influx of settlers from the East.

The vigilantes

This massive influx of people all hoping to make a fortune, combined with the poor living conditions, caused enormous problems of law and order. Gambling and drunkenness were rife, since miners had few other ways of relieving the boredom and misery of their lives. In the early days the miners assumed personal responsibility for settling disputes through their own rough-and-ready courts. **Claim-jumping** – the act of stealing a man's claim to a mine after he had discovered gold – and murder thrived in communities where there was no formal system of law enforcement.

Some mining towns set up their own **vigilante groups** to keep law and order (see also page 75). These were gangs of men who took it upon themselves to uphold the law and to punish those who broke it. Sometimes, however, the men in these groups were almost as bad as the lawbreakers they were supposed to be controlling. So-called courts tried cases quickly and often in an atmosphere of anger or hysteria. Justice was rarely fair. Witnesses were intimidated and there was no appeal. In the absence of permanent prisons, death sentences were carried out immediately. Frequently, vigilantes behaved no better than lynch mobs, spreading terror wherever they went. More seriously, vigilante committees sometimes took over the government of towns. This happened twice in San Francisco, in 1851 and 1856, after California had become a State with its own elected government.

Source F

▲ An engraving showing hangings by vigilantes in San Francisco in 1851. The men being executed had been accused of starting fires in the city.

Map legend:
- —— Oregon trail
- − − − California trail
- —— Santa Fe trail
- - - - Mormon trail
- ······· Old Spanish trail
- — — Gila River trail

Mountain and Plateaux Region

Mining areas 1849-1874

▲ The location of mining activity in the American West, 1848–74.

What were the benefits of the discovery?

In spite of all its drawbacks, there is no doubt that the discovery of gold in California in 1848, and then later in Nevada and Dakota, was an important turning point in the development of these regions, and in the economic growth of the USA as a whole. Some of the benefits were that:

- It increased the supply of money and encouraged more investors, both at home and abroad, not only to expand the mining industry but also to develop light industry. San Francisco became a successful shipbuilding and flour-milling centre.
- It stimulated the rapid growth of San Francisco which soon rivalled New York as a financial centre.
- It ensured that when the railroad across North America was built in the 1860s, it would pass through California rather than Oregon.
- The wealth created helped to give the USA a leading role in world trade. This made the purchase of essential materials for development possible (eg steel for the construction of railway lines).

QUESTIONS

1 In what ways did (a) the mountain men and trappers and (b) the US Government help the westward migration of settlers in the 1840s?

2 Which groups of people moved to Oregon and California in the 1840s? Why did they go?

3 Look carefully at Source A on page 31.
   a What impression does this painting give of life for travellers on the Oregon Trail?
   b How accurate do you consider this impression to be?

4 'The discovery of gold in California in 1848 was an important turning point in the history of the American West.' Do you agree with this statement? Think about the **social**, **political** and **economic** effects of the discovery of gold.

SUMMARY

▶ Mountain men and animal trappers were great pathfinders. Their trails, once mapped were used by thousands of migrants

▶ The great migration – the first mass East-West trek – began at Independence, Missouri in 1843.

▶ Life on the trails was hard, with final destination unknown.

▶ The Californian gold rush began in 1848. As the number of forty-niners then rose, disorder and racial disharmony followed.

▶ Gold in the West brought untold wealth to only a few, but the rush stimulated economic activity in the region.

The Mormons were very different from the farmers and gold-seekers. Unlike them, they lived a **communal life**, both on the trail and when they arrived in the West. This means that they shared everything and owned nothing themselves. They were also a religious group who were forced westwards by persecution. There is little evidence that 'manifest destiny' played any part in their motives for moving. On the contrary, they wanted to escape from the USA altogether. Their remarkable success in settling in the West enabled them to develop into a religious body that is still significant in the USA today.

Who were the Mormons?

Their official name, as registered in 1831, was **The Church of Jesus Christ of the Latter Day Saints**. Their beliefs and way of life made them distinctively different from other Americans.

The founder of this religious movement was **Joseph Smith**, the son of a poor farmer in Vermont. Smith claimed that, in 1823, he had seen a vision of an angel called Moroni. The angel told him to go and find some gold plates hidden in a hillside called Cumorah in Palmyra, New York State. The plates then had to be kept hidden for four years. Smith found the plates and, four years later, secretly translated the inscriptions on them while hidden from view behind curtains. The translation was subsequently written down in the *Book of Mormon* and published in 1830. Eleven witnesses were finally allowed to see the plates in order to verify their existence and the truth of their contents.

The *Book of Mormon* describes the migration to America of the tribes of Israel: the Nephites, Jaredites and Lamanites (from whom, it said, the Indians were descended). The book also tells of the coming of Jesus Christ to America after his Resurrection. There was constant warfare between the tribes. A tribesman called Mormon and his son, Moroni, were the only survivors. Mormon subsequently wrote down the events on the gold plates. Members of the church were commonly called 'Mormons' after him.

▲ Joseph Smith, the founder of the Mormon church.

Source A

On the evening of the . . . twenty-first of September (1823) . . . I betook myself to prayer . . . While I was thus in the act of calling upon God, I discovered a light appearing in my room, which continued to increase until the room was lighter than at noonday, when immediately a personage appeared at my bedside, standing in the air, for his feet did not touch the floor . . . He had on a loose robe of most exquisite whiteness . . . Not only was his robe exceedingly light, but his whole person was glorious beyond description, and his countenance truly like lightning . . . He called me by name, and said unto me that he was a messenger sent from the presence of God to me, and that his name was Moroni; that God had a work for me to do.

▲ The calling of Joseph Smith, taken from the 'Testimony of the Prophet Joseph Smith', in the *Book of Mormon*.

Kirtland, Ohio, 1831

In just a year after the publication of the *Book of Mormon*, Joseph Smith had made a thousand converts. Missionaries were travelling throughout America and to Britain to convert more. Numbers grew quite rapidly. One of Smith's first objectives was to carry out God's will by building a 'holy city' or **Zion** (City of God) in America. It was not going to be an easy task. Everywhere the Mormons went their homes were attacked and some individuals were tarred and feathered (including Joseph Smith, himself, in 1832). Kirtland, Ohio was Smith's first chosen site in 1831. At first everything went well in spite of some outbreaks of violence. In 1833 the Mormons began to build their first temple. Their numbers grew and they prospered. Smith even founded a bank which was used by Mormons and non-Mormons alike. However, non-Mormons became uneasy as they began to be outnumbered. Then, in 1837, during a general financial crisis, the Mormon bank collapsed. Both Mormons and non-Mormons were dissatisfied with Joseph Smith but the anger of the non-Mormons was far greater. The Mormons were driven out of Kirtland. A very bitter Joseph Smith led his people to Missouri where missionaries had already established a small community (see map on page 41).

Missouri

The story there was little different. The Mormons were not welcome from the beginning. Apart from the antagonism caused by their religious differences, the authorities were suspicious of the Mormon leaders who believed in the communal ownership of property. Mormons also came from the north where many people were opposed to slavery. Because the landowners in Missouri owned slaves, they did not welcome anyone who might speak out against slavery. Violence broke out and increased, especially as the non-Mormon communities knew the Mormons had formed a sort of secret police force called the **Danites**. They believed the Danites were planning to win the support of the Indian tribes.

Some Mormon beliefs and practices
- *No individual ownership of property.*
- *In return for total obedience the Mormons would be God's chosen people both on earth and in heaven.*
- *As many people as possible should be converted to Mormonism.*
- *A man could have more than one wife.*
- *The leaders of the Mormon Church should also have political power, and thus have authority over everyone.*

Source B

. . . As we could not associate with our neighbours [who were many of them the basest of men and had fled from the face of civilized society to the frontier country to escape the hand of justice] in their midnight revels, their Sabbath breaking, horse-racing and gambling, they commenced at first to ridicule, then to persecute us. Next an organized mob assembled and burned our houses, tarred and feathered, and whipped many of our brethren, and finally drove them from their habitations. This proceeding was ignored by the government, and although we had deeds for our land and had violated no law, we could obtain no justice.

▲ Joseph Smith describes the persecution of the Mormons in Missouri.

QUESTIONS

1 Look carefully at Source B. Describe Joseph Smith's attitude to the non-Mormon settlers in Missouri.

2 Are any of his complaints reasonable?

3 How does this source help to explain the hostility shown to the Mormons by the other settlers?

4 In what ways were the Mormons different from other settlers at that time?

But little more than two years ago, some two or three of these people made their appearance on the Upper Missouri and they now number 1,200 souls. . . Each autumn and spring pours forth its swarm among us, flooding us with the very dregs . . . Well-grounded complaints have been already made of their corrupting influence on our slaves . . . We are told that we of this country are to be cut off and our lands taken over by them.

▲ Extract from the *Missouri Intelligencer* and Boon's *Lick Advertiser*, 10 August 1833.

The Mormon leaders were imprisoned but their persecuted flock was led away to safety by **Brigham Young**, one of the leaders who had not been imprisoned because he was out of Missouri when the trouble broke out (see map on page 41).

Nauvoo, Illinois 1839

This time the destination was Illinois. Here Smith, now released from prison, began to build his 'holy city'. It was named Nauvoo and was built around the existing village of Commerce. Smith was determined that the Mormons would not be driven out. He obtained a charter from the state government of Illinois. This allowed them to have their own army and also to make their own laws. It was a way of creating a state within a state. At first he was successful because the two rival political parties in the state government wanted the support of the Mormons. By 1842 the Mormon army was 2,000 strong. However, this degree of independence, supported as it was by military might, began to alarm the non-Mormon communities, particularly as the laws of the Illinois State were frequently ignored.

Some Americans also feared that the Mormons intended to take over the USA. This fear was increased when Joseph Smith announced his intention of running for President.

▲ An engraving of a polygamous Mormon family. Smith claimed the practice of polygamy (having more than one wife) was the will of God. Non Mormons and even many Mormons were disgusted by this, and feared a Mormon population explosion, although only the leaders could afford to keep large families. Smith had ten wives by 1843.

In June 1844 Smith and his brother, Hyrum, were imprisoned after ordering the destruction of a printing press operated by a breakaway group of Mormons. On 27 June a mob of non-Mormons attacked the jail in Carthage where the brothers were being held. They were both shot and killed.

Why was hatred of the Mormons so widespread?

Many people of different religious beliefs went to settle in the American West to escape persecution. None aroused such strong feelings of hatred as the Mormons. There were many reasons for this unpopularity:

- Their rapidly increasing numbers, thanks to their energetic conversion policy.
- Their leaders' belief in polygamy. This was hated as much as slavery by some Americans.
- The close relationship between the leadership of the church and politics. If Joseph Smith had had his way, the laws of the Mormon church would have been the laws that everyone had to live by whether they were Mormons or not.
- Like the Jews in the Old Testament of the Bible they believed that they had been especially chosen by God . They even referred to non-Mormons as 'Gentiles'.
- They believed that, as God's chosen people, they had to be seen to be special. They showed this by being a particularly hard-working community of people. This made them very prosperous, which was resented by people who struggled but without the same degree of success.

The Mormons in crisis

The death of Joseph Smith in June 1844 could have brought about the end of the Mormons as a mass movement. Leaderless, persecuted by non-Mormons and internally divided over the issue of polygamy, it must have seemed likely to their enemies that the Mormon threat had been removed. Small breakaway groups left Nauvoo with their own chosen leaders. Joseph Smith III, the son of the founder, rejected his father's teaching on polygamy and started the Reorganized Church of Jesus Christ of the Latter Day Saints in Independence, Missouri.

However, Joseph Smith's vision was kept alive by **Brigham Young**, Smith's faithful follower who assumed the leadership of the remaining 15,000 Mormons after his death.

Brigham Young: profile of a leader

Like Joseph Smith, Brigham Young came from Vermont. He learned the trades of a glazier and a carpenter and was converted to the Mormon faith in 1832. His abilities were soon recognized and he became a trusted member of the Quorum of the Twelve Apostles that governed the church. He was trusted by the Mormon leadership and allowed to take charge of a mission to Britain where he later claimed to have converted 9,000 to the faith. He gained the respect of the Mormon community when he led them out of Missouri at the time when the rest of their leaders were in prison. At the time of Smith's murder, he was in Boston organizing his campaign for the presidency. He returned quickly to Nauvoo and assumed the leadership. His influence on the future of the Mormons was enormous as the next pages show.

QUESTION

Look back over the reasons for the hatred of the Mormons. Think about the following reasons in your answer: **social**, **political**, **economic**, **religious**.

He proved to be just the right man at the right moment. He had the answers to their problems, the ability to carry them through and the personal qualities that earned him the respect and total devotion of the faithful.

Where did Young take the Mormons next?

Just before his death Joseph Smith knew that the Mormons would have to leave Nauvoo. He had begun to negotiate for land outside the USA. In 1844 vast territories in the West still belonged to Mexico.

Brigham Young agreed that there was no future for the Mormons within the USA and wherever there were 'Gentiles'. Helped by the writings of those first trailblazers – Young chose the Great Salt Lake located in the southern Plateaux region between the Rockies and the Sierra Nevada, an area considered to be an uninhabited desert.

The demands on Young were enormous. He had to organize the safe movement of 15,000 men, women and children on a journey of approximately 2,250 kilometres. In 1845, when he began to make plans, the route was still difficult and dangerous. Every household set to work to build wagons and prepare themselves for the journey. But anti-Mormon hostility broke out on a huge scale in the spring of 1846. Houses and people were attacked. So the decision was made for the advance party to leave ahead of schedule. Young's plan was to establish a camp on the banks of the Missouri River and plant crops to support the rest through the winter. By the time the first group had reached the camp called **Winter Quarters**, many of the travellers were already suffering from disease or exhaustion. Some had died.

Salt Lake City

During the winter and early spring, Brigham Young prepared his people for the journey across the Great Plains. Families were divided into groups of a hundred and then sub-divided into fifties and tens, with each ten led by a captain. They were taught how to travel in columns and form circles. The daily routine was very strict. Anyone breaking the rules was punished.

The long wagon train struggled over the Plains following the Oregon Trail until it reached South Pass. In June 1847 Young located the trail through the Rocky Mountains. On 23 July Young's wagon reached the head of a pass. He looked out over the valley. Disregarding the advice of Jim Bridger and others who warned him that nothing would grow in such a wilderness, Young decided that this was their destination. Later this land would form part of the State of Utah.

Source F

At 5 a.m. the bugle is to be sounded as a signal for every man to arise and attend prayers before he leaves his wagon. Then cooking, eating, feeding teams etc till seven o'clock, at which the camp is to move at the sound of the bugle . . . No man to be permitted to leave his wagon unless he obtains permission from his officer . . . At 8.30 p.m. the bugle to be sounded again at which time all to have prayers in their wagons and to retire to rest by nine o'clock.

▲ From Brigham Young's orders for the journey across the Great Plains. These were in the journal (daily record) of the journey written by William Clayton, one of the travellers.

Source E

The fever prevailed to such an extent that hardly any escaped from it. They let their cows go unmilked. They wanted for voices to raise the psalms on Sundays . . . Here at one time the digging got behind; burials were slow, and you might see women sit in the open tents keeping the flies off their dead children, some time after decomposition had set in. But the worst part of the journey was yet to come.

▲ From an account by a US Army officer who provided medical help at one of the Mormon camps on the way to Winter Quarters.

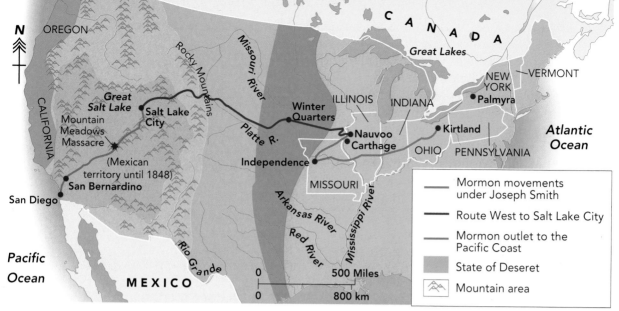

▲ **The journeys of the Mormons and the state of Deseret.**

The Mormons in Utah today still celebrate 24 July as **Pioneer Day**, the day that the first group of their ancestors reached the end of their trek West and arrived in what was to become Salt Lake City, Utah.

How did Young make the desert bloom?

Brigham Young's organization, determination and discipline had got the Mormons to the Great Salt Lake, but his true qualities of leadership and courage were yet to emerge. He had to make this desolate wilderness habitable; then there was his flock of thousands, many of whom must have shared the feelings of his sister-in-law (see Source G). It is a tribute, perhaps, to Young's amazing qualities that they accepted his word and continued to follow his authoritarian leadership. The experience of the journey probably helped here. In Mormon history it was compared with the Old Testament Exodus of the Jews led by Moses. It was a great boost to the morale of the faithful after the setbacks of persecution, internal division and argument.

The Mormons finally had the opportunity to fulfil the destiny that Joseph Smith had planned for them. They could build their 'holy city' and live as a community.

▶ **An extract from the diary of Brigham Young's sister-in-law, Harriet, describing her first reaction to the Salt Lake valley.**

Source G

My feelings were such as I could not describe. Everything looked gloomy and I felt heart sick. Weak and weary as I am, I would rather go a thousand miles farther than remain in such a desolate and forsaken spot as this.

Brigham Young's instructions to the first Mormon settlers

- Work parties were to be set up to look for timber and fresh water supplies (although the area seemed to be an empty desert).
- Fields were to be planted and irrigation channels dug to prepare for the remaining groups arrival.
- Work was to begin on the 'holy city'.
- There was to be no private ownership of land or natural resources. Land was to be distributed but had to be farmed successfully or it would be repossessed. Water for irrigation was to be strictly rationed and provided at appointed times.
- Shops, houses and other buildings were later to be allocated by Church leaders.
- One tenth of all earnings (a tithe) was to be paid to the Church.

Every aspect of their lives were governed and dictated by the Church and its leaders. Brigham Young's purpose was to establish a Mormon state. He set about the task with great energy.

How would the Mormons survive?

The first months in the Salt Lake valley were extremely hard. Many died of cold and hunger in the winter and grasshoppers devoured the crops in the following summer. Settlement was not easy as these problems returned time and time again. Brigham Young knew that the future of the Mormons depended on the size of the population and on its ability to be completely **self-sufficient**. To some extent, these two went together. He encouraged Mormons to come from Britain, Europe and other parts of America to the Salt Lake valley. A **Perpetual Emigration Fund** was set up to help them. Handcarts were designed so they could haul their belongings along the trail. Many of these emigrants had skills in manufacturing which would promote self-sufficiency. There were soon ten other communities in the Salt Lake Valley. Young himself played his own polygamous part in raising the population. His 23 recorded wives gave birth to 49 children – much to the horror of the rest of the USA.

Young also used every opportunity to expand the economy of his 'state':
- Following the gold rush of 1849, he set up supply depots and workshops where travellers going to California could re-stock and repair. He also charged tolls to cross Mormon territory.
- When the railroad was being constructed across the West to Sacramento, California, he negotiated with the Union Pacific Railroad Company for the railway to pass north and south of Salt Lake City. This helped the development of trade.

An independent Mormon state?

Young's hope was that an independent state called **Deseret** would make the Mormons completely secure. It was a vast territory stretching as far as the Californian coast,

Source H

Some views of Brigham Young

A devout believer, but more especially a lion-hearted man of iron will, an organizer and the founder of a commonwealth.
Written by H. E. Bolton, Young's biographer.

Outside observers claimed that his leadership was characterized by dictatorship, arrogance and suspicion.
From H. S. Commager, *The West*, 1976.

He has been the brain, the eye, the ear, the mouth and hand for the entire people.
From a speech made at Young's funeral in 1877.

There is a batch of governors and judges and other officials here shipped from Washington, but Brigham Young is King.
A visitor to Utah after 1860.

because Young wanted the state to have an outlet to the sea This hope soon died.

In 1848 the Salt Lake Valley was included in the territory handed over to the USA by Mexico (see maps on page 72). This meant that Young now had to apply for his community to be admitted to the USA. It was decided to make Deseret a territory rather than a state but with the name of Utah (after the Ute Indians who lived there). This meant that, as a territory, the Mormons would not be independent of the USA. Brigham Young became Utah's first governor, but the Mormons were deprived of their outlet to the sea and became subject to laws of the USA. But they chose to ignore these and continued to live by their own laws. Government officials were attacked. Young used his secret association – the Danites – to remove opposition from outside and within the Mormon ranks.

Crisis in Utah

In 1857 the US Government responded to the events in Utah by sending out its own Governor, along with troops to protect him.

The situation became very tense as the Mormons also had their own army. War seemed possible. Matters came to a head when a wagon train of settlers from Missouri was massacred at **Mountain Meadows**, Utah. The Mormon leaders claimed that Indians had carried out the massacre. Many people believed that the Danites were responsible. The Government, afraid of full scale war, agreed to allow the Mormons to practise their religion and to live in their own way but their territory was not allowed to become a State while the Mormon church continued to encourage polygamy.

So when Young died in 1877, the Mormons were still surrounded by hostile Americans. In one way, it must have seemed that the upheaval of moving to the Salt Lake had been for nothing. But, by the time of his death, Salt Lake City was a prosperous city, and the power of the Church was firmly established through the system of government that Young had devised. Many of the foundations that he laid, such as the communal ownership of land still remain today.

After the death of Brigham Young, the US Government launched a more vigorous attack on polygamy. In 1890 the Mormons finally abandoned polygamy and Utah was admitted as a State to the USA by 1896.

SUMMARY

▶ **1830** Joseph Smith wrote the Book of Mormon and began to gain followers.

▶ **1831–7** The Mormons settled in Kirtland, Ohio and began to increase and prosper.

▶ **1837–8** The Mormons were driven from Kirtland by persecution. They settled briefly in Missouri.

▶ **1838** The Mormons moved to Illinois and built the city of Nauvoo.

▶ **1843** The start of the migration to Oregon. Smaller numbers went to California.

▶ **1844** Mormon persecution in Nauvoo. Joseph Smith murdered. **Brigham Young** became leader.

▶ **1846–7** Mormons were driven from Nauvoo and trekked to the Great Salt Lake.

▶ **1848** Mexico handed over land to the USA including Salt Lake valley. Utah became a territory of the USA but resisted US laws and officials.

▶ **1896** Utah became a state.

3.4 EXERCISE

1 *'That the entire body of Saints did not break up may be credited to the skills of the newly appointed prophet, Brigham Young.'*
Do you agree with this judgement? Write a detailed answer. Before writing, gather your information by making notes under these headings:
  a The problems faced by Young in 1844
  b Young's personal qualities
  c Examples of his actions that illustrate these qualities
  d His aims and how far he achieved them.

  Use your notes to arrive at your own view of Young's importance to the Mormons.

2 Study Source H:
  a What can you learn from these comments?
  b Using your knowledge, say how far do you think these comments are fair?

3 If the Mormons were to successful, why were they so hated by non-Mormon Americans?

TRAINS TO CROSS A CONTINENT

On 10 May 1869, at Promontory Point in Utah, a spike was tapped in to join two stretches of railway line. The spike was special: it was made of gold. The railway line was even more special: it now ran right the way across the USA. Thus it became possible for people to travel from East to West and back by the fastest form of transport then known.

Later in this chapter you will find out how this great railway came to be built, and what effect it had on American life. But first we will look at the transport and communications system that existed before the railway came: the steamboats and stage coaches, the Pony Express and the telegraph. Their inadequacies will help to explain why, in the end, transcontinental trains became essential.

▲ A steamboat called the *Little Eagle* on the Missouri River in Kansas.

4.1 What transport preceded the railways?

Transport was vital in 19th century America. The settlers and their folks back East liked to keep in touch by mail. Supplies had to be sent West, while farm produce was sent the other way. As communities grew in size, law enforcement officers and judges had to be able to move quickly from place to place; and the US Government in Washington needed fast access to its western territories.

Steamboats

The first forms of transport to the West were steamboats that sailed along the major rivers such as the Mississippi and the Missouri as well as several of the rivers in the West. By 1846, there were 1,190 steamboats operating along these rivers carrying millions of dollars worth of freight (goods) inland. But the steamboats were slow and there was growing need for faster forms of travel and communication.

This demand came partly as a result of the discovery of gold in California. By the early 1850s there were also a number of US army posts in the West which had to be supplied with food and ammunition. The demand was met at first by stage-coaches, freight wagons and the Pony Express. The Government was so keen to improve communications that it provided money to improve the roads on which the wagons travelled.

▲ A stagecoach and team of horses preparing to leave a Wells Fargo office.

In very cold weather do not drink liquor (alcohol) when on the road; because you will freeze twice as quickly when under its influence . . .

Do not keep the stage waiting. Do not smoke a strong pipe inside the coach – spit on the leeward side.

Don't swear or lop over neighbours when sleeping.

Expect annoyances, discomfort and some hardship.

▲ Advice to travellers in the *Omaha Herald*, 1877.

How was land transport made quicker?

Enterprising business people were prepared to invest money to meet the need for improved transport. The most famous was the **Wells Fargo Express**. By 1850 it was possible to travel by stage-coach from Independence, Missouri to Salt Lake City in Utah. In 1851 the route was extended to California.

In 1853 **William B. Wadell** and **William H. Russell** were given a contract to carry military supplies to army posts in the West. From this grew a large and successful freight wagon business. By 1858, the firm had 3,500 wagons and 40,000 oxen. An equally successful freight service was begun by **Ben Holladay** who became known as the 'stage coach king' of the West. When he sold out to Wells Fargo in 1866 his stage lines covered 8,000 kilometres. These businesses were helped when the government decided to provide money for the improvement of wagon roads.

This improvement must also have helped **John Butterfield** to establish his overland mail service in 1857. Butterfield was a 'self made man' who began work as a freight wagon driver. His overland service carried mail a distance of 4,480 kilometres from St Louis (in the East) to San Francisco (in the West). In 1856 he was given a $600,000 government contract to set up the service. By 1858 he had built 141 way stations, constructed bridges, bought 1,500 horses and 250 coaches. He employed 800 men. The demand for speed, however, continued. It took almost three weeks for these mail coaches to cross the continent. Could a faster method be found?

What was the Pony Express?

On 3 April 1860 the Waddell and Russell freight company started a new and daring enterprise. They started to employ young men (see Source F) to ride between relay stations across the continent at breakneck speed carrying the mail in specially designed saddle bags. As one rider approached a relay station the next had to be ready to ride. It took only minutes to hand over the mail bags. This service was called the **Pony Express**. The company bought 500 ponies and employed 200 young men who travelled between 150

► A painting by Frederic Remington of the Pony Express showing the change over at a relay station.

Source **E**

Across the endless dead level of the prairie a black speck appears against the sky, and it is plain that it moves . . . In a second or two it becomes a horse and rider, rising and falling – sweeping toward us nearer and nearer – growing more and more distinct, more and more sharply defined – nearer and still nearer, and the flutter of hooves comes faintly to the ear – another instant a whoop and a hurrah from our upper deck, a wave of the rider's hand, but no reply, and man and horse burst past our excited faces and go swinging away like a belated fragment of a storm!

▲ The author, Mark Twain, was excited to see a Pony Express rider in action. He included this decription of the experience in his novel, *Roughing It*, first published in 1872.

relay stations following the Oregon and California trails. They could cross from St. Joseph, Missouri to Sacramento, California in ten days, calling at Salt Lake City, Utah. Riders had to brave the rough countryside, the harsh climate and sometimes hostile Indians. They were not allowed to swear or drink and were issued with a Bible, a shotgun and a rifle.

The Pony Express lasted for only two years. On 22 October 1861 the first **telegraph** message was sent across America, so there was no further need for an express mail service. But in this short time these daring young men had captured the American imagination. Back East in St Louis, stories abounded of riders outrunning Indians, and being eaten by hungry wolves. One story told of a rider who arrived at a relay station dead in the saddle, his body riddled with Indian arrows but still desperately protecting the mail. Pony Express riders soon passed into the folklore of the West (see Source E).

Source **F**

Young, skinny, wiry fellows, not over 18 years of age. Must be expert riders, willing to risk death daily. Orphans preferred. Wages $25 a week.

▲ An advertisement for Pony Express riders in a San Francisco newspaper in 1860.

QUESTION

Read Source E. Is Mark Twain creating a romantic image of the Pony Express rider or is he genuinely impressed? Explain your answer using the Sources and your knowledge.

Whilst the stage-coach and freight firms were getting underway, some business people were already anxious to see the development of a transcontinental railway network. In 1853 the US Government paid $150,000 for a survey to be made for possible railway routes across America to the Pacific. By 1860, railways had been built with money from groups of investors from the east coast to the Mississippi. In the West, railways were being built in Texas.

Why did the US Government want a railway?

The building of a transcontinental railway was important to the government for the following reasons:

- Many people had migrated beyond the Mississippi to Oregon and California and there was a need to take government, law and order to these territories and to create a sense of national unity.
- The Government wanted to benefit from the wealth that was being created by the discovery of gold. There were possibilities of opening trade links with countries such as China. This would mean using ports on the West coast of the USA.
- The railway would also be another way to fulfil the belief in 'manifest destiny', as it would make migration into the uninhabited areas of America much easier.

The two main political parties in the USA were the Republicans and the Democrats. In its election campaign of 1860, the Republican Party promised the nation a transcontinental rail link. In July 1862 Congress passed the **Pacific Railways Act**. By the terms of this Act two companies were set up to build such a railway – the **Union Pacific Railway** (in the East) and the **Central Pacific Railway** (in the West). The Union Pacific would build as far as Missouri and then branch on to the Plains. The Central Pacific would start in Sacramento and build eastwards. Both companies were given land and 30-year government loans.

What problems were encountered in building the railways?

Money was a major problem. Government grants were not sufficient and early attempts by the Union Pacific Railway to encourage Americans to invest their money in the scheme met with a disappointing response. The land grants from the Government were used as security, at first, for loans. Later, some of this land was sold to settlers. This meant that the Central Pacific Railway then had to find other backers to provide a large amount of the capital that was needed.

The building work itself was extremely hard.

Source A

▶ Chinese workers building a section of the transcontinental railway through the Sierra Nevada in 1867.

Workers suffered the extremes of cold and heat and the dangers of landslides. These dangers were particularly great for those working in the mountains of the Sierra Nevada and the Rockies. Labour shortages were another problem. In 1863 the Central Pacific Railway Company solved this difficulty by using immigrant Chinese labour. Between seven and ten thousand additional workers were brought from China. When the Government set the final deadline for the completion of the railway (10 May 1869), Irish labourers were also brought in to speed up the work. The Civil War (1861–5) slowed down progress, but the final deadline was met, at Promontory Point, and a railway now ran from one end of the USA to the other.

4.3 What impact did the railways have?

The opening of the first transcontinental railway from Sacramento to St. Joseph began a great wave of railway building similar to the 'railway mania' which took place in Britain in the 1840s. Four more major railways were built across the continent soon afterwards and branch lines to farther-flung communities were also constructed. Between 1850 and 1890 railway mileage grew from around 20,000kms to over 324,000kms, most of it in the West.

Why were some people unhappy about the railways?

The railway network was regarded as a national triumph by many but some people were not happy:

- Many businesses were caught by the competition between the railway companies, especially over the price of carrying freight.
- Some farmers were unhappy because they

► Transport across the USA. The routes of the transcontinental railways in the last quarter of the 19th century.

believed that the railway builders were only interested in making profits, rather than providing a good service.

- The days of the stage-coach, the freight wagon and overland mail were almost ended by the railways, although they still operated a service from the rail head to more remote settlements on the Plains.
- The railways made a huge difference to the lives of the Indians. Not only did they bring a large number of settlers who wanted their land, but they also disturbed the buffalo. It became a new pastime to shoot the buffalo through the window of a moving train whenever a herd was seen.

What were the benefits of the railways?

- People could now travel more easily across the continent: government officials, law enforcement officers, and judges as well the relatives of those who had already migrated to the West.
- Essential supplies such as seeds, machinery, timber, food, raw materials and manufactured goods could be carried to the new settlements from the East.
- Agricultural produce could be carried more cheaply to distant markets.

- The railways encouraged the growth of cities in the West, such as Denver, Dallas and Los Angeles.
- The railway-building boom coincided with the USA's industrial revolution, and helped to make the USA the world's leading industrial power by 1890. In that year its rail network was bigger than the whole of Europe's, including Britian and Russia.
- The foreign trade of the USA was helped by the railways and this helped to increase the wealth of the country.
- The railway network provided the opportunity for thousands of new settlers to travel to the West and for the cattle industry to grow up on the Plains. So the railways prepared the way for the second major phase of migration on to the Great Plains.

In the next two chapters we will look at two of the groups in this second phase who came to the Plains at the same time during the 1860s: the **cattlemen** from the South and the **homesteaders** (farmers) from the East.

SUMMARY

▶ Steamboats on major rivers provided passenger and freight transport.

▶ **1850–1** Wells Fargo stagecoaches were introduced.

▶ **1853** Wadell and Russell's freight wagon company began. A Government grant was provided to survey for a railway across the American continent.

▶ **1857** Butterfield's Overland Mail was introduced.

▶ **1860** The Pony Express was started.

▶ **1861** Transcontinental telegraph was introduced.

▶ **1862** Pacific Railway Act – work began on the Union Pacific/Central Pacific railway.

▶ **1869** First transcontinental railway completed.

QUESTIONS

1 Explain why it was so important to set up the different methods of communication that you have read about in this chapter.

2 The stage coach and the Pony Express have come to be part of the romantic image of the West:
   a In what ways was life for the men involved hard and dangerous?
   b Use what you have learned to explain why they might have been romanticised.

3 Why was it necessary to find another system of transport in the West?

4 Money was raised for the railway in two ways:
   a Government land grants
   b Private investment

   Explain how these two helped the development of the railways. Was one of these more important than the other? Explain your answer carefully.

CHAPTER 5

CATTLEMEN AND COWBOYS

Source **A**

▲ **Texas Longhorns. These were a very sturdy breed of cattle that could survive by themselves in all kinds of weather conditions on the trail and on the Plains. They were not prime beef, which meant the meat was not popular at first in the East. This painting by Frank Reaugh is called** *The Herd.*

In Chapter 3 you read about Charles Frémont's report of 1844 on the West (see page 30). In it he thought that the Great Plains, far from being a 'Desert', could be transformed into a highly prosperous area. From the 1830s until the end of the Civil War in 1865, the cattlemen from the South blazed the first trails to the north, but it was not until the 1870s that the first cattle ranches on the Plains were established, proving Frémont correct. From 1867 to the 1880s the consequent boom or 'bonanza' in the beef trade made many ranchers rich. It also gave work to a group of men who soon came to symbolize all that was exciting and dangerous about life on the Plains. These were the cowboys and this was the era of the famed 'Wild West'.

5.1 How did the cattle industry begin?

Longhorn cattle were first brought to America from Europe at the end of the 15th century. By the early 19th century, cattle ranching was firmly established in Mexico. The cattle grazed freely on the **open range**. This means that the Mexican ranchers did not keep the cattle within fenced areas. Cowboys called **vaqueros** were employed to look after the cattle. At this time Mexico owned the huge area called Texas, but in 1836 the Texans rebelled against Mexican rule and set up an independent republic. The Mexican ranchers left Texas leaving their cattle behind. The Texan farmers duly claimed these as their own and branded them with their own mark.

Beef in plenty

At first, Texan cattle ranches were quite small. Beef was not a particularly popular meat so the animals were slaughtered mainly for their hides and for tallow (fat used in candle-making). But during the 1850s beef became more popular so its price began to rise, making some Texas ranchers quite wealthy.

In 1861 Civil War broke out in the east between the northern and the southern states of the USA (see page 13). Texas fought on the side of the Confederate (southern) armies. The war ended in defeat for the South and it destroyed the economies of the southern states, including that of Texas. But during the five years of the war, the Longhorns had survived on the open range and had continued to breed. It is estimated that, in 1865, there were about five million Longhorns in Texas, but they were worth little unless they could be taken north, where there was an increasing demand for beef. By 1865 railway construction across America was well underway. Texas ranchers were promised ten times the local price if they could get their cattle up to the railway. Their eventual success, as you will see, was the result of the work of a number of determined individuals.

5.2 Who was behind the 'beef bonanza'?

Joseph McCoy has the reputation of starting the 'beef bonanza' (the boom in the beef trade), although there were other groups of traders who had also realized the potential of the trade in beef. McCoy was a livestock trader in Chicago. His aim was to make Chicago the centre of the meat trade in the East and to make himself a lot of money in the process by taking a commission (a percentage payment) on each head of cattle. This was not an easy task. Farmers who had already established homesteads (farms) in Kansas objected to the Longhorns crossing their land because they carried a tick (a kind of insect) that did not harm the Longhorns but killed other animals. So a quarantine ban had been imposed. Cattlemen travelling north met with fierce opposition. Knowing of this hostility, cattle ranchers were reluctant to bring their animals to Kansas.

What was the 'real McCoy'?

McCoy knew that the railway companies were keen to carry more freight on their trains. The Kansas Pacific Railway undertook to route its new railroad past a frontier village which came to be known as Abilene. There McCoy paid for the building of a hotel, stockyard, office and bank. This became one of the first **cow towns**. Abilene was near the head of an established trail across the Plains which lay to the west of the Kansas farmlands – the **Chisholm Trail**. This had been made as a supply trail during the Civil War by a trader called Jesse Chisholm. Apart from the difficulty of crossing the Red River it was mostly a wide, flat trail. This meant that the cattlemen could drive their herds to the railhead at Abilene without any hostility from the farmers. Later, the trail branched out to the cow towns of Ellsworth and Dodge City.

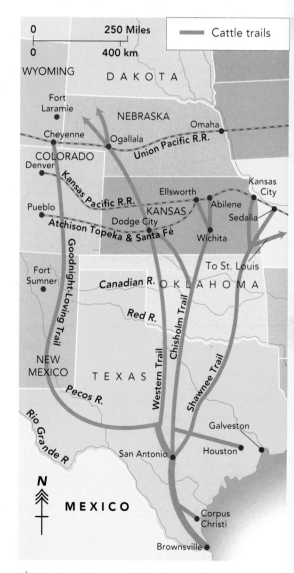

▲ **Cattle trails across the Great Plains.**

▲ **Joseph McCoy, Chicago cattle dealer.**

▲ **Charles Goodnight.**

▶ **The cow town of Abilene, Kansas in 1879. Between 1867 and 1880 half the cattle transported along the Kansas Pacific Railway came up the Chisholm Trail, and departed for the eastern cities from Abilene, Ellsworth and Dodge City.**

In 1867 McCoy spent $5,000 on advertising material and riders, promising the Texas ranchers a good price for their cattle in Abilene. By the end of 1867, 35,000 head of cattle had been driven along the Chisholm Trail to Abilene. It was the beginning of the 'beef bonanza'. McCoy was seen to be man of his word. In 1868 one cattleman bought 600 head of cattle in Texas for $5,400 and sold them in Abilene for $16,800. Between 1867 and 1871, he sent around two million head of cattle to Chicago. His reputation for reliability gave rise to the expression 'the real McCoy'.

The Goodnight-Loving trail

Charles Goodnight was a Texan who returned from the Civil War in 1865 to find that his stocks of cattle had risen significantly. He was born in Illinois but grew up in Texas and began his cattle business by gathering together a small number of cows as payment in kind for work done for other ranchers. By 1860 his herd was 180 strong. When he returned from the Civil War, it had grown to 5,000. The animals were of little use, however, unless they could be sold.

Goodnight knew that the Government needed food for army outposts. Also, by the 1860s, some Indian tribes were beginning to be located on reservations (see Chapter 8). These depended on meat supplied by the US Government. In 1866 Goodnight decided to drive his herd, which now numbered 8,000, to Fort Sumner (see the map on page 51). There were no farmers in this area of the Plains to cause any trouble. On the other hand, the route passed through Indian territory.

Goodnight teamed up with another rancher, Oliver Loving, who already had experience of droving and together they blazed the **Goodnight-Loving Trail**. This lay to the west of the other trails on the edge of the High Plains. Goodnight had

worked out that each steer would need thirty gallons of water during the journey and ten acres of prairie grass. Shortages of water and hostile Indians made the journey very hard. In spite of this, Goodnight continued to use his trail as the Government wanted more and more beef in the 1870s to supply the Indian reservations.

Ranching on the Plains in the 1870s

Some cattlemen, weary of the dangers and difficulties of the long drives from Texas, began to establish ranches on the Plains. There was, after all, plenty of grass and the Longhorns could graze on the open range as easily there as in Texas. However, the Government grants of land were only for those who intended to grow crops and set up permanent homes, so the cattlemen abandoned their ranch houses whenever the cattle moved on. At this stage, the cattlemen were like squatters on the land.

John Iliff

John Iliff was a rancher with an eye to the main chance. He began as a prospector looking for gold when it was discovered in Colorado in 1859. Then he opened a store on the Oregon Trail in Wyoming, selling supplies to travellers. Once he realized how sturdy the Longhorns were, he began to buy cattle. To begin with, these were bought from Charles Goodnight at the end of his first drive in 1866. Soon Iliff's herd numbered 35,000. He then sold beef to the rail companies that were building the transcontinental railway in 1867. After 1868 he obtained Government contracts to supply meat to the Sioux reservation.

Iliff also tried to capture eastern markets by producing a better quality beef through cross-breeding the Longhorn with Herefordshire cows from England.

Source **D**

Dudley and John W. Snyder promise to buy 15,000 head of steers of the ages of two and three years next spring, and to drive the cattle to Colorado from Texas and deliver to John Iliff . . . in July 1878. Upon delivering the steers [young male cattle], John Iliff agrees to allow sixteen dollars per head for the three-year-old steers and twelve dollars for the two-year-olds per head.

▲ An extract from a contract to buy cattle from Texas cattlemen.

Source **E**

. . . for furnishing delivered at any station on the Denver Pacific Railroad, the beef, flour, potatoes, cabbage, turnip onions, oats, corn and hay required by the track-laying forces during the construction of the said road.

▲ Extract from a beef contract won by John Iliff in 1869.

Source **F**

◀ John Iliff.

Source **G**

State/ Territory	Cattle 1860	Cattle 1880
Kansas	93,455	1,533,133
Nebraska	37,197	1,113,247
Colorado	none	791,492
Wyoming	none	521,213

▲ Figures for the cattle industry on the northern Plains. Taken from census figures for 1880.

QUESTIONS

1 Make a list of the reasons why there was an increased demand for beef in the second half of the 19th century.

2 Why were McCoy, Goodnight and Loving and Iliff so important to the development of the cattle industry?

By the 1880s people back in the East had developed a very romantic image of the American cowboy. This had been encouraged by travelling wild west shows in which so-called cowboys performed clever or daring feats and by articles in magazines such as *Harper's Weekly*. The cowboy appeared skilful and glamorous, facing danger with courage and always coming out of it unscathed. He was invariably depicted as a white American. This image has stood the test of time, reinforced by artists such as Frederick Remington and by the Hollywood films. But how near to reality was this image?

By the end of the 19th century, cowboys may well have dressed and behaved to live up to their popular image, but in their heyday, from about 1867 until the 1880s, this was not the case. Although they were mostly young men, their origins were very mixed. Some were Negroes and Indians, others were of Mexican or Spanish origin. Many were former Confederate soldiers, desperate for work. A lot were drifters and some were criminals on the run (see Source B). They enjoyed the sense of freedom that came from riding the range. They were rarely married. Most cowboys were employed on a seasonal basis at particularly busy times of the year and were not paid much then. Even when they were not being paid, a lot of them stayed on the ranch. They were given their food and lodging in return for doing jobs around the ranch, especially during the winter.

Life was hard. They lived in the primitive bunk house on the ranch and were strictly disciplined – drinking, swearing or gambling could lose them their jobs. Their clothing evolved from the demands of their work and the need for protection against the weather.

Source A

◀ A sculpture in bronze by Frederic Remington (1902) called *Coming through the Rye*. It shows a group of cowboys riding into town. Remington was fascinated by the courage, speed and skill of the cowboy.

'The bandana. The handkerchief (usually red) which was worn around the neck, and for use as a mask. When the cowboy rode along behind the herd of cattle, he pulled the handkerchief up over his nose and mouth to protect him from the dust'.

'The hat (stetson) was made of felt. The broad brim protected the wearer from the sun and was an umbrella in rainy weather. In winter it could be pulled down over the ears and tied – giving protection from frostbite'.

'The saddle was the cowboy's throne – its bumps and contours grew to fit the owner's body. A man might gamble away his money, horse or chaps, but he would put his saddle on his back and return home on foot'.

A laviat or lassoo.

' The "chaps" were an overgarment like a pair of trousers with a cut-out seat. Many were made of the shaggy skin of a bear, goat or sheep. They were also to withstand the thorny vegetation, the cutting north wind, and to protect the legs from chafing during a long ride and in the case of a fall'.

' All cowboys wore high heeled boots. The heel and arch were so constructed that the foot and leg were comfortable when riding. Spurs were worn at all times'.

▲ **The cowboy – his clothing and equipment. Extracts from *The Long Drive* by Everett Dick.**

Source *B*

Not all cowboys were clean-living, hard working young men who lived a lonely life on the trail and had a good time when they came to town. Some cowboys were rotten. John Hardin was one of them . . . John Wesley Hardin was the son of a Methodist preacher . . . while driving 1,200 Longhorns on the Chisholm Trail toward Abilene, Wess shot two Indians, one for demanding a toll. A little further along the trail he got into a row with some Mexican cowhands. He settled that sqabble by spilling the blood of five of them all over the prairie.

▲ Royal B. Hassrick, *The American West*, 1975. The cowboy's way of life was useful to those who wanted to avoid the law! (See also page 77.)

Source *C*

Most of them were Southerners and they were a wild, reckless bunch. For dress they wore wide-brimmed beaver hats, black or brown with a low crown, fancy shirts, high heeled boots, and sometimes a vest (waistcoat).

▲ A description of a cowboy's dress by a cowboy, 'Teddy Blue'.

The life of the cowboy

The cowboy's life was, in some respects, similar to that of the Indian's. His daily routine was totally bound up with the cattle, just as the Indian's was concerned with following the buffalo. As the Longhorns grazed on the open range, the cowboy spent much of his time in the saddle, roaming the Plains. His days were long, his work was very hard and often dangerous.

Winter

Winter was the most boring time of year. Cowboys were sent out to ' line camps' on the borders of where the cattle were grazing. Usually they were sent in pairs but often alone. Their task was to patrol the grazing areas which were covered in snow to ensure that the cattle were not in difficulty. They also had to watch out for wolves or other wild animals that might attack the herd. In the freezing cold, blizzardy conditions, their shelter was often only a tent with a corral (a small paddock) for the horses. When the snows melted in early Spring, their job was to ride the range to rescue cows that had sunk in the mud or been caught in swollen streams.

Round up and branding

Two of the busiest times in the cowboys' year came when the cattle were rounded up. One was in the spring when the young calves were separated from the herd to be branded. The second was in late summer when the cattle to be driven north were gathered.

Ranch owners branded their cattle because, although each ranch had defined territory, the cattle from different ranches mingled on the open range. The cowboys from several ranches usually joined together in the round-up. It involved looking for their brand and 'cutting out' their animals and this needed skilful riding. In spring, the newly born calves usually stayed close to their mothers so it was not difficult to locate new stock for branding. The cowboy had to lassoo the young animal to bring it down for the hot branding-iron to be applied to its rump. It was then let free to return to its mother. Even so, the cattle could roam over millions of hectares of land, so the rounding-up and branding could take two to

▶ Robin May, *History of the American West*, 1984.

Source D

▲ *Roping a Steer* (young male) by Charles Russell. Russell worked as a cowboy for a time on a ranch in Montana. When he was working as an artist, he lived the 'typical' cowboy life to the full.

Source E

The best paid job out of season was the wolfer – killing wolves. The best method was to track a wolf to its lair when it was slowed down by food. Then one cowboy crawled into the lair holding a candle and a six gun. As the gun's explosion often blew the candle out, the job was not for the nervous.

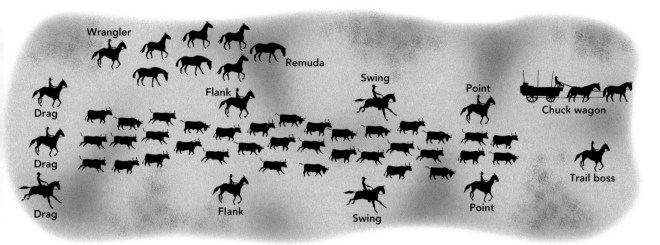

▲ The long drive.

three months. During this time, the cowboys lived in camps out on the range, based around the truck wagon where the cook prepared their meals.

Rounding up the fully grown steers for market was also dangerous. Because they had roamed freely they were like wild animals. Their long horns were an extra hazard for the cowboys.

The long drive

From 1866 until the mid 1870s, the cowboys had to drive the cattle from Texas to the cow towns located on the railway – a journey which could take up to two months. Later, when ranches were set up on the Plains, this was reduced to about 35 days. Even so, it was a hazardous journey. The average herd was made up of about 2–3,000 head of cattle, but herds could be as small as 600. The largest recorded herd was 15,000 head of cattle.

When prices were high, the cattle ranchers wanted to sell as many beasts as possible. This placed a great responsibility on the cowboys because the loss of only a few would cost the rancher a lot of money. Usually, the rancher hired a team of cowboys for the drive. Sometimes, especially in the early days, they led the team in person. On average, there were 250 – 400 steers to each cowboy.

The long drive, however, was a major challenge for all the cowboys. Their day began at around 4.00 a.m. and ended well after dusk. If it was a cowboy's turn to stand on guard during the night, he would have to work for almost 24 hours. Within the team, each man had his own responsibilities (see diagram).

- The **trail boss** had overall responsibility. He got up at about 3.30am and made sure that there was enough food before rousing the men for the day's work. He gave the orders, checked the herd and rode ahead to find water. He made the decisions about where the camp would be made and generally took care of the welfare of his men. He rode at the front of the herd on the so-called chuck wagon.
- The **pointers** were also experienced drivers. They led the herd when the trail boss had ridden on to look for water or a camp.
- The **swing** and **flank men** rode at the side and rear to keep the herd loosely together.
- The **drag men** were in the rear. This was the worst job because they became covered in dust from the herd in front.
- The **wranglers** were the youngest and most inexperienced cowboys on the drive. They were kept at the back and were used for carrying messages up and down the line. They also had to look after the **remuda** – the spare horses that were kept together in the rear of the herd. Each cowboy was allocated five or six horses.

What were the hazards of the long drive?

Loss of sleep was, not surprisingly, one of the biggest problems that cowboys faced daily. Other problems they faced included the following.

- **Stampedes** were most likely to happen in the first few days of the drive when the animals were restless and anxious to get back to their home pastures. The slightest sound would set them off. The herd could stampede several times in one night and travel many kilometres before they could be stopped. This could only be achieved by the cowboys driving the stampeding animals into a circle. It was a very dangerous job. Stampeding cattle also lost weight which would lower their value at the railhead.
- The **weather** and the **landscape** could be hostile. Cowboys were exposed to blistering hot winds and torrential rain and hail storms. There were also dangers at river crossings, especially if the rivers had been swollen by heavy rain or if there were quicksands. The Red River, for example, on the Chisholm Trail was often flooded.
- **Indians** posed another threat. Some of them were friendly and allowed the herds to pass on payment of a toll – usually a number of head of cattle. Others were hostile. In 1870, for example, Cheyenne Indians stampeded a valuable herd and drove them off.

Source F

While I was looking at him, this steer leaped into the air, hit the ground with a heavy thud, and gave a grunt that sounded like that of a hog. That was the signal. The whole herd was up and going – and heading right for me. My horse gave a lunge, jerked loose from me, and was away. I barely had time to climb into an oak. The cattle went by like a hurricane, hitting the tree with their horns. It took us all night to round them up . . . next morning we found ourselves six miles from camp.

▲ **Charles Goodnight describing his experience of a stampede on the long drive (undated).**

▼ **This painting by Frederic Remington shows Longhorns being stampeded by a flash of lightning.**

Source G

- **Rustlers** (animal thieves) were a danger as the herd drew nearer to the railway. They drove off part of the herd and overlaid their own brand on that of the owner. Then they took the steers into town and sold them.
- **Settlers** clashed frequently with cattlemen. There was hostility in Kansas to the Longhorns (see page 51). Others complained that they trespassed on their land. This was difficult to avoid because before 1874, when barbed wire was invented, the boundaries of the homesteads were marked only by a ploughed furrow – no barrier to cattle. Sheep herders also laid claim to grazing lands on the Plains and resented the cattlemen.

What happened at the end of the trail?

When the herd was near to the cow town the cattle were allowed to graze to fatten them up before meeting the dealer. Then the cowboys with their herd rode through the town firing their guns. It was the end of weeks of gruelling work, anxiety and danger. Now they would get their reward!

There were no shortages of places to relieve these carefree men of their money (see Source I). Drunkenness and brawls were common. Sometimes there were gun fights. By the 1870s, families were settling in these towns and in 1872 the people of Abilene finally banned the cowboys. Dodge City, Newton, Elsworth and Wichita became journey's end.

Source H

The wild ones [Indians] would stampede our horses and try to get away with them. The friendly ones would run them off at night and come back the next day to get a reward for returning them. . . . There was scarcely a day when we didn't have a row with some settler. The boys took delight in doing everything they could to provoke settlers. The settlers paid us back with interest by harrassing us in every way they could think of. The boss was arrested twice in one day for trespassing.

▲ **Bill Poage, a cowboy on a long drive, describes some of the problems of the trail.**

Source I

The bar-room, the theater, the gambling room, the bawdy house, the dance house, each and all come in for their full share of attention. . . . Such is the manner in which the cowboy spends his hard-earned dollars.

▲ **Joseph McCoy describing the activities of cowboys in Abilene.**

QUESTIONS

1 Why were young men attracted to the life of a cowboy?

2 What were the drawbacks of the cowboy's work and style of life?

5.4 Why did the cattle trade rise and fall?

The boom years

The cattle trade boomed from 1867 until the early 1880s. During these years the railway network was extended and the development of refrigerated railway carriages meant that cattle could be slaughtered before transportation to the cities of the East and West. So larger quantities of beef could be sold and transported to markets at home and, later abroad. The 'bonanza' attracted a lot of interest abroad, bringing fortune hunters to the USA from Britain and Europe.

The problems of land-ownership, however, still existed in 1880. The law still required the owners of land to farm it and to live on it for

◀ Cattle barons. These large ranch owners formed the Prairie Cattle Company in 1885, which owned over 150,000 cattle. Joint-stock companies like this helped the cattlemen to increase their profits.

a set period of time. This did not suit the cattlemen whose livestock continued to graze freely. Some of the richer ones tried to get around this by having their ranch-hands claim the land and then live on it. They then 'bought' it from them, much to the disgust of the homesteaders. But by 1880, there was much more public land available as the Indians were being removed from their traditional 'hunting grounds' to be located on **reservations**. So the ranches on the Plains flourished.

Why did the boom end?

This boom did not last long. In the last twenty years of the 19th century the beef trade almost collapsed. There were several reasons for this:

- Some farmers were beginning to experiment with other, less sturdy breeds of cattle, such as the Herefords from Britain, which could not live so easily on the open range.
- There was a diminishing supply of grass and still a very large number of cattle due to overstocking, as more and more cattlemen started businesses when prices were high. In 1883 there was a drought

and unusually high summer temperatures which ruined the grass.

- After 1885 the demand for beef began to fall and so did the prices. It was no longer profitable to keep huge herds.
- The final blow to the cattle trade was dealt by the severe winter of 1886–7. Cattle and cowboys died in the snow, ice and freezing temperatures. There was no point in re-stocking to former levels, so the time had come for a new approach.

How did wire and windpumps help?

It now seemed sensible for smaller units to produce smaller quantities of better quality beef. The animals could not be allowed to wander freely, but how were they to be contained and where would the water supplies come from? Two inventions helped to answer these questions.

- In 1874 **J F Glidden** invented **barbed wire**. This enabled large areas of land to be fenced cheaply. At first, this did not help the cattlemen because the homesteaders cut the fencing, claiming that they had been cut off from their water supplies. The second invention helped to solve this problem.

- The **windpump** (windmill) used the strong winds across the Plains to power a pump that would draw water from underground. It meant that cattle ranchers were no longer obliged to site their ranches with immediate access to water. This invention was also a great boon to farmers as the prairie soil was so hard that it was very difficult to dig wells.

The windpump and cheap fencing meant that the homesteaders began to replace their furrow boundaries with barbed wire. So the ranchers had to do the same, which brought about the end of the open range.

How did the cowboy's role change?

The establishment of fenced ranches on the Plains had a great impact on the role of the cowboy. The long drives were a thing of the past and round-ups were much smaller affairs. Fewer cowboys were needed. For those that remained, their jobs – mending fences, for example – became more mundane and predictable. The wild and free age of the cowboy was at an end except when it was exaggerated and dramatized as entertainment for eastern audiences. But if the cowboys became a feature of the legend of the West, so did another important group in this second phase of emigration: the homesteaders. In the next chapter you will find out about them.

Source *B*

▲ *The Fall of the Cowboy* by Frederic Remington.

SUMMARY

▶ Abilene, Dodge City and the other cow towns were lawless playgrounds for the cowboys.

▶ **1880–5** The peak period of the cattle industry; after this the demand for beef fell.

▶ **1886–7** A very severe winter reduced cattle stocks, accelerated the growth of ranches and the inventions of barbed wire and windpumps – thus signalling the end of the cowboy era.

5.5 EXERCISE

1 Describe in detail the changes in the cattle industry from 1860 to 1886 using the information and sources.

2 Explain why each of the following was important in the development of the cattle industry. Were any of these more important than the others?
   a the Civil War
   b the railway
   c enterprising individuals such as McCoy and Goodnight
   d the cowboys?

3 Look back over the paintings and the sculpture that are included in this chapter:
   a What impression do they give of the cowboy?
   b Why were artists so fascinated by the cowboys?
   c In your opinion, was this fascination justified? Explain your answer.

CHAPTER 6

HOMESTEADERS ON THE PLAINS

Early Americans saw the Great Plains as a vast desert, unfit to live in and impossible to cultivate. By the mid-19th century that view was changing. Even before the cattlemen and their herds began to cross the Plains from the South, farmers were moving in from the East and taking root. By the 1850s they were living in Kansas and Nebraska; in the 1860s they were moving into South Dakota. After 1889 even Oklahoma – once designated as Indian territory by the US government – was opened up by the white man. All these areas were part of the **Low Plains** (see map).

The 1870s saw the greatest number of settlers moving on to the Plains and setting up new homesteads (farms). By 1880 they had infiltrated the much drier region of the **High Plains** too, as far as Colorado and Montana. All these homesteaders went West to seek a better life, but wherever they settled on the Plains they had to face great hardships. As you will see in this chapter, even though they belonged to the second great phase of migration, they had to be just as intrepid as the trailblazers who had gone before them.

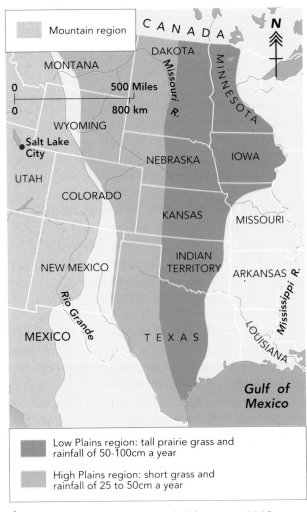

▲ **The areas of the Plains settled between 1860 and 1890.**

6.1 What made the homesteaders go West?

Where did they come from?
Most of the migrants were from eastern states such as Illinois and Wisconsin. After 1865, when the Civil War ended and the Negro slaves were given their freedom, some Negro families also ventured West.

Foreign immigrants joined those searching for a new life on the Plains. These came from England, Ireland, Europe, Scandinavia and Russia. The rate of immigration into the USA increased from half a million in the 1830s to 5.25 million

Source A

The number of foreign-born immigrants on the Plains 1860–80

(% of total population)
Kansas	13 %
Nebraska	20 %
Dakota	32 %

by the 1880s. Once in the USA, these immigrants tended to be concentrated in certain areas of the Plains (see Source A). Immigration and westward migration in general were both accelerated by the building of the railways in the 1860s.

Almost all of the homesteaders travelled West in families. This was important in the development of the Plains because the women and children helped to create a stable and orderly society at a time when the only other strong influence was that of the cattlemen and cowboys. An example of this is the effect of family life on the cow town of Abilene (see Chapter 5).

What was the attraction of the Plains?
Like the trailblazers, the homesteaders moved West for a variety of motives:
- Some had already moved into the Mississippi valley but found it too heavily populated for them to make anything of their land, even if they could buy some. So they moved on. The family of Laura Ingalls Wilder, who wrote the *Little House on the Prairie* stories, had done this.
- Some moved to escape from poverty. This was certainly true of some of the foreign immigrants such as the Irish.
- Some, such as the Russians and the Jews, wanted to escape from religious persecution.
- Others simply went West from a sense of curiosity and adventure or to build a political career in the new territories.
- Once people had moved West, their letters home sometimes encouraged relatives to follow.

- People were strongly influenced by articles in magazines and newspapers which created attractive images of the West (see the poster on page 10).

Who encouraged potential settlers?
Officials in the various territories of the West developed immigration programmes as early as 1855. They were aware of the importance of an expanding population. It would have **social** effects in creating communities, towns and cities; **economic** effects by producing and selling goods, as well as encouraging the growth of the railways. Above all, it would have important **political** consequences. Once a territory had a population of 60,000 it could apply to to be admitted as a full state of the USA. This would give its politicians a lot of power in organizing their own affairs within the state. So it was in the officials' interest to go to great lengths to attract settlers.

Source C

I saw vast areas of unimproved land, rich as that on the banks of the far famed Nile. We saw land before us, land behind us, land at the right hand, land at the left hand . . . oceans of land all ready for the plough, good as the best in America, and yet lying without occupants.

▲ **The editor of the *Kansas Farmer* wrote this after a journey in the West in 1867.**

Source B

Ma, you can see just as far as you can please and almost every foot in sight can be ploughed.

▲ **An extract from a letter, written in 1875, by a young settler in Nebraska to his mother back in the East.**

Source D

The capacity of our territory for raising immense herds of cattle and for the production of large crops of corn, wheat, oats, rye, barley, buckwheat, potatoes, melons, fruits and vegetables, demonstrate the ability of our country to sustain a dense population.

▲ **An official from Dakota encouraging immigration there by making extravagant claims for the fertility of the land in 1869.**

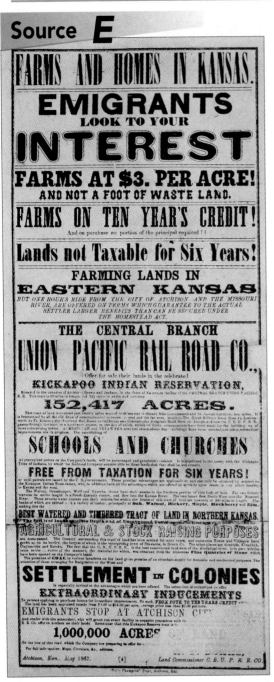

▲ A Union Pacific railway advertisement for land.

The **railway companies** were also anxious to attract settlers. They needed to sell the land that the Government had given them to help to finance the building of the railway. But, much more importantly, they needed people to travel on the railways and to produce goods that they could carry. Settlers would also need essential supplies – timber, seed and farm machinery. This would develop their freight business. So the railways also advertised at home and abroad.

They lured settlers with offers of credit, long term loans at low rates of interest and delayed-repayment packages in order to allow them time to become established. Added to this was the offer of 'exploration' tickets to enable prior inspection of land, free transport to the nearest railway town to their purchased land and accommodation along the way.

In 1875 the Santa Fe Railroad invited 225 newspaper editors from the USA and abroad to visit the West at the company's expense. In 1882 half a million promotional posters were translated into Swedish, Dutch, Danish and Norwegian. It was all very hard to resist!

● **Free Land** was certainly the major attraction and in this the **US Government** had a very important part to play by making free land available to prospective farmers (**the Homestead Act**) in a way that would encourage migration. In the 1860s, the Great Plains remained the one massive tract of land in the USA that was not inhabited by Americans. In order to fulfil the ideal of 'manifest destiny', settlement of these open spaces had to be achieved. The politicians also tried to give an equal opportunity to poor people to become landowners.

The Homestead Act, 1862

You already know that land was sold by the railway companies at special prices to attract settlers. An earlier Act of 1841 allowed settlers to buy 160 acres of land at a very low price per acre. Finally in 1862 the Government in Washington assigned lands in Kansas, Nebraska and Dakota for settlement and passed the Homestead Act. The land was again divided into 160 acre units or homesteads which could be acquired free of charge, apart from a small administration charge to file the claim.

By the terms of this agreement, the homesteaders were obliged to build a house on the land and live there for five years. After that time, they received the title deeds to the land. If they wanted the deeds quickly, they could buy the land after six months.

In 1873 the Government extended this Act with the **Timber Culture Act**. This offered 160 acres of land free provided that at least 40 acres of it were planted with trees. Later, the requirement was reduced to ten acres. Any potential settler, including foreign immigrants, could claim this land under both these Acts.

What was wrong with the Homestead Act?

Once the scheme was in operation, some critics said that the amounts of land were too small to support a family and enable the homestead to thrive. After 1875, when the available land was extended to the High Plains, this was probably true. Colorado and the eastern part of Wyoming were much drier and the land was potentially less fertile. It was likely that, in this area of the Plains, not all the land could be ploughed. Settlers there quickly found that some of the land was better suited to rearing animals – cattle or sheep. They also had better farm machinery by this time, which enabled them to bring larger areas under cultivation. Under these circumstances, 160 acres were insufficient.

It was also possible to obey the letter of the Act but ignore its intention. Land speculators had many employees applying for free land. This meant that they could acquire large quantities of land very cheaply, which was not what the government had intended. You have already seen how the cattlemen used this ploy to acquire land on the Plains. Land speculators later resold the land at higher prices.

What was good about the Homestead Act?

- At the time when it was passed, there seemed little likelihood of people settling beyond the eastern edges of the Plains. Given the fairly simple farm implements that the homesteaders used at the time, 160 acres was thought to be manageable.
- After 1873 it was possible for a homesteader to acquire as much as 480 acres of land if he claimed the 160 acres under each of the three Acts, including that of 1841. This made homesteads bigger and more likely to make a profit.
- The Government accepted the criticisms of the size of homesteads. The Homestead Act was later amended to allow holdings of 640 acres. Title deeds could also be handed over sooner. In 1877 it also passed the **Desert Land Act** which enabled farmers to buy 640 acres of land in areas where rainfall was a particular problem and schemes of irrigation were necessary.
- Whatever its shortcomings, the Homestead Act played a significant part in encouraging settlement on the Plains. The amount of land on offer, 2.5 million acres, was enormous. In the early 1870s, thousands of farmers acquired free land. In 1871–2, 9,000 claims were made in Kansas alone. By 1885–7 this rose to 43,000 claims. By encouraging the development of transport links, especially the railways, the Government also made migration possible at a much faster rate.

SUMMARY

- ▶ In the 1850s the first homesteaders arrived in Kansas and Nebraska mainly from the East.
- ▶ The **Homestead Act** of 1862 granted settlers 160 acres of free land under certain conditions. This was extended by the **Timber Culture Act** of 1873.
- ▶ The **Desert Land Act**, 1877 made more land available in dry areas.
- ▶ In the 1870s the territories and railway companies advertised widely to encourage further immigration.

Homesteaders must have travelled to their new land full of optimism and excitement. Their doubts had been allayed by the promises of the advertisements and by those who claimed that the 'rain followed the plow'. Many were to get a shock when they arrived at their destination and tried to cultivate the land. Those who had been farmers back in the East clearly thought that they would simply move to a new place and then carry on as before. They took with them the seed and the farming implements that they were used to, only to find that, in many areas of the Plains, they were hopelessly unsuited to the task before them.

Source **A**

▲ **A homesteader family outside its sod dug-out in 1892.**

What were the problems for the farmer?

- **A lack of water**. There was insufficient rainfall to allow wheat to grow successfully. The hot sun also baked the earth hard, which made the ground extremely difficult to plough. For those who were not fortunate enough to be near to a river or creek, this also meant that water was hard to obtain as wells were very difficult to dig.

- **A shortage of building materials**. On arrival, those who had travelled by wagon, used the parts of the wagon to build a makeshift home. But, again, if they were not near to a river where there were trees, then they had to make their homes of the only raw materials available – the hard baked Prairie earth. **Sod houses**, sometimes little more than a lean-to, were built all over the Plains especially in Minnesota, parts of Nebraska and the Dakotas. Families were still living in these in the late 1880s. A newspaper reporter commented in 1878 that he had seen 'settlers in dug-outs and sod shelters as contented and happy as a preacher, as comfortable as a king'. It is debatable whether the occupants would have agreed. The main advantage was that these houses cost almost nothing to build.

- **Extremes of weather**. Howling winds were a constant feature of the Plains. These would be scorching hot in summer and bring hailstorms and torrential rain which destroyed crops and contributed to the homesteaders' hardships. Periods of drought, such as those in 1860 and 1880, were disastrous.

- **Prairie fires and plagues**. Both could destroy crops in no time at all. Sudden prairie fires were common and were spread rapidly by the wind. Farmers were also often hit by plagues of grasshoppers, such as the one in 1871, that devoured the crops. Further plagues of grasshoppers struck in 1874 and 1875. The swarms were so thick that they stopped trains on the Union Pacific Railroad!

- **Protecting the crops**. In the early years, farmers had neither the materials nor the money to put fences around their property. All they could do was to mark the perimeter of their land with a furrow. This meant that wild animals could wander on to their land. Once farmers moved onto the High Plains, they were more frequently in the path of the cattlemen. Crops were easily destroyed by the Longhorns and this caused friction with the cattlemen (see Chapter 5).

Source B

They [the grasshoppers] came upon us in great numbers, in untold millions, in clouds upon clouds, until their fluttering wings looked like a sweeping snowstorm in the heavens, until their dark bodies covered everything green upon the earth. In a few hours many fields that had hung so thick with long ears of maize were stripped of their value and left only a forest of bare yellow stalks that in their nakedness mocked the tiller of the soil.

▲ The editor of the *Wichita Eagle*, describing the effects of a grasshopper plague in the 1870s.

QUESTIONS

1 Make a chart to summarize
  a the reasons that drove people to leave their original homes
  b the reasons why they were drawn to move West.
In your opinion, were the factors that drove settlers away from their homes more important, equally as important or less important than those factors that drew them to the Plains?

2 Read Source B. How helpful is this source in showing the seriousness of a grasshopper plague?

6.3 A tough life for women

Women had a difficult time living on the Plains. The sod houses were impossible to keep clean. They were infested with bugs and insects; dusty in hot, dry weather and dripping with water when there was a storm. The only good thing about them was they could not be destroyed by prairie fires. They were also very unhealthy without proper sanitary arrangements or clean, running water. Illness, especially among the children, was common so the mother of the family had to nurse sick children using her own remedies (warmed up urine was a common cure for earache!). A doctor could be many miles away. Infant death from diphtheria was common. Women also died in childbirth because of the lack of medical care.

Source A

▲ Part of the daily life of a housewife on the Plains. This woman has collected cow or buffalo dung for fuel.

Source B

I have fought bedbugs and fleas all summer, scrubbed rough plank floors and mingled my tears with the suds

▲ A comment by a settler, Mrs Henry Gray to Cora Beach, a writer in *Women of Wyoming* in the late 1870s.

Source C

It was not wholly the fault of the sod house that contagious diseases were common. The common drinking cup, the open dug well, the outdoor toilet [or no toilet at all] shared the blame with the lack of ventilation and crowded quarters of the sod house. . . . The floor of a dugout, or sod house, was commonly of clay dirt. It was not possible to scrub or disinfect it of the millions of germs that found a breeding place in the dirt trodden underfoot.

▲ Dr Cass G. Barns' opinion about the sod houses that he saw in Nebraska in 1878. He and his wife had just arrived to live on the Plains.

Source D

. . . done my housework then made fried cake, squash pies, baked wheatbread and corn bread, cut out a nightdress and made it. . . . I am very tired.

▲ A diary entry for one day in the life of a woman in Kansas in 1873.

Why did women have to be versatile?

Everyday items which might have been taken for granted before were missing. Substitutes had to be found for soap, sugar, and coffee. Every scrap of cloth was used either to remake clothes for smaller children in the family or for bedding. Women on the Plains became very skilled at making patchwork quilts. If they kept sheep, they would spin and weave their own woollen cloth. They also had to be teachers. Until small townships grew up nearby the children could learn to read and write only if their mothers taught them.

Since there were so few trees, fuel for cooking was another problem. As in so many other aspects of Plains life, women had to use what was available. Dried buffalo or cow dung, as the Indians knew, was an effective substitute. Gathering this was often the woman's job. It was heavy work. To survive, women had to be physically strong. They also had to be able to plough and help in the fields when they were needed. Even when goods were available to them, some families were too poor to buy them, so replacing everyday things like pots and pans was impossible for many.

It is not surprising that diaries and childhood memories of that time often emphasize the loneliness and fear of life on the Plains – especially for the women left alone for days when their husbands went hunting or to the nearest town for supplies. Women sometimes went mad from loneliness, despair and the constant howling of the prairie winds.

Did Plains life improve over time?

As more settlers arrived on the Plains, small communities were established. This made life easier. There were 'neighbours' near enough to visit from time to time. A general store carried almost everything that families needed, as long as they could afford to buy. A school was built for the children and the church provided an opportunity for people to meet socially as well as for religious services. By the 1880s some of these towns were organizing cultural activities. In 1885, for example, the town of Cheyenne, at the end of the Kansas Pacific Railroad, was entertained by the Covent Garden Opera Company on tour from England!

This does not mean, however, that all the problems of surviving on the Plains had been solved for everyone.

Survival depended largely on farmers being able to adapt to the climate of the Plains. To some extent, their success also depended on where their land was located, as the fertility of the soil varied from area to area. When they first arrived, the main aim was to cultivate enough land to provide food for the family. Each year, a little more land was put to the plough in order to create a surplus for sale. As farmers made money from their crops, they bought new or better farm machinery which, in turn, added to their success. Some farmers also discovered at an early stage that their crops would need to change. Settlers in Kansas and Nebraska, for example, who recognized that the land was more suitable for growing wheat than corn (maize), increased their yields many times. Those who moved to the High Plains and were successful had realized that it was more appropriate to keep livestock than to grow crops.

Did all homesteaders eventually succeed?

Unfortunately, the problems outlined earlier made it impossible for some farmers to make ends meet. In desperation, they were obliged to mortgage the property that they had obtained free under the terms of the Homestead Act. Sadly, this did not always work out either and many lost their land or became tenants on land that they had previously owned. Between 1889 and 1893, 11,000 homesteads were repossessed in Kansas alone and the number of tenancies in Kansas and Nebraska doubled in the same period. Many of these changes were caused by the severe droughts of the 1870s and 1880s. During this time, many families almost starved. The situation was so desperate that even attempts by the US Army to distribute relief were inadequate.

What inventions and techniques were effective?

The homesteaders who succeeded were adaptable and benefited from a number of new techniques and inventions that helped to combat many of the problems that they had faced at first:

- **New crops**. Apart from the changes in crops already mentioned, American

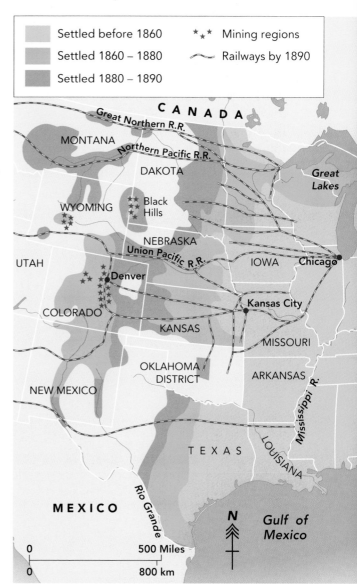

▲ The stages of migration on to the Plains.

farmers benefited from the experience of immigrant settlers. The Russians had brought **Turkey Red wheat** with them to the USA. This was a particularly hardy type of wheat which was well suited to the Plains. The farmers who changed to planting this seed produced good yields.

- **Better machinery**. The difficulty of turning the hard prairie soil led to the invention of a particularly strong plough by **John Deere**, which could cut into the earth and turn it ready to cover the planted seed. It became known as the **sod-buster**. As time went by, better farm machinery – reapers, binders and threshing machines – became available. These could be transported out to the farmers by the railway.

- **Fencing the land**. This had been difficult until Joseph Glidden invented **barbed wire** in 1874. This provided a cheap and effective way of stopping stray animals or the stock of the cattlemen from crossing their territory. It was a source of friction with the cattlemen because they claimed that the homesteaders' fences cut them off from their water supplies.

- **Water**. Homesteaders had sometimes needed to dig thirty feet down in order to locate water and make a well. The invention of the windpump was a great boon to those who could afford to have one. Farmers also developed a new means of conserving moisture in the earth. This was known as **dry farming**. It required farmers to plough their land when there had been heavy rain or snow to enable the moisture in the soil to be preserved. A thin layer of dust was put on the surface to stop evaporation of the moisture and a field was left fallow (empty) to allow this process to work in preparation for the following year's crop.

These methods did not benefit everyone because not all farmers had the money to invest. It is probably true to say that the homesteads that succeeded were those that made steady progress from the beginning.

▼ **The Oklahoma Land Rush, 27 April 1889.**

Source A

6.5 What was the 'Sooner State'?

On 22 April 1889 the US Government opened up another two million acres of land in the former Indian territory of Oklahoma. A month after the announcement had been made, thousands of people, some already homesteading in less promising areas, massed at the starting point, living rough or in tents until the appointed hour. At midday on 22 April, a gun was fired to signal the start of the 'rush'. Between 50,000 and 100,000 people in wagons and on horseback dashed to stake their claim to land. Inevitably, some cheated and hid themselves on their stake the night before. They came to be known as 'sooners' and Oklahoma was dubbed the 'Sooner State'. In 1893 a further six million acres of land were released. Almost 60 years earlier, this land had been promised to the Cherokee Indians for ever. By the end of the 19th century, the West was changing fast and, as you will see in the next chapter, it was also becoming less wild.

SUMMARY

► Many homesteaders had to live in insanitary sod houses.

► In the 1880s migration into the High Plains area increased.

► New inventions, new techniques and new crops brought success to some homesteaders.

► The Oklahoma Land Rush of 1889 brought two million acres of land on to the market. Six million more acres became available in 1893.

6.6 EXERCISE

1 a Why did artists paint pictures like this (Source 1) when they were not depicting the truth?

 b Why were pictures such as that in Source A on page 66, not so common in the East?

2 a Compare and contrast the role of women on the Plains with that of the Indian women who had lived there before they arrived.

 b Which of the two do you consider to have had the better way of life?

3 'Short term hardship for long term gains'. Was this true for all the homesteaders on the Great Plains? Use your knowledge and the sources to help you to answer this question.

Source 1

▲ A painting called *The Western Farmers' Home*. It was painted for the benefit of Americans in the eastern states.

CHAPTER 7

HOW WILD WAS THE WEST?

The words 'wild' and 'West' always seem to go together – thanks largely to the impression made by Hollywood's cowboy films. This wildness might well have been exaggerated but the enforcement of law and order in the West really was difficult. The West attracted all kinds of people, for all kinds of reasons. Some were honest and serious-minded. But others went West to avoid or break the law.

So why was there disorder in the West?

- The huge area, and slowness of transport made 'policing' the West difficult.
- Mining camps and cow towns were centres of lawlessness.
- Vigilantes (self-created policing groups) used violence and created terror.
- Gunslingers and gangs dominated many areas.
- Conflict on the range frequently broke out between cattlemen and homesteaders.

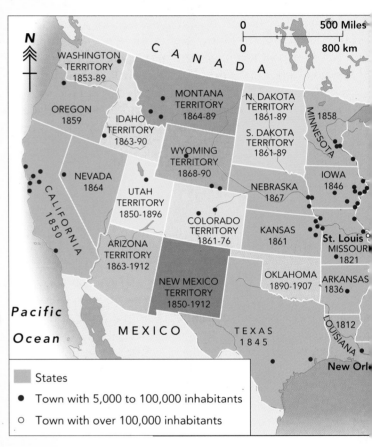

▲ **The states and territories of the United States of America by 1870.**

7.1 Why was the West hard to police?

You have already seen in Chapter 1 how the US system of government worked. When the Civil War ended in 1865, most of the lands west of the Mississippi were still **federal territories**. These territories were divided up into towns and counties. They were controlled by the Federal Government because there were not enough inhabitants to raise the money in taxes to pay for their own services. The government was responsible for roads for example, and enforcing law and order.

There was, however, a shortage of reliable law enforcement officers to keep order over such a huge area of land. When the Federal Government sent officials to govern the territories, lawmen were also sent.

▲ *The Vigilantes*, a painting by Rufus R. Zogbaum (1885).

Source **B**

Five men were caught robbing a gambler and were given thirty-nine lashes each, but three were then accused of murder and an attempted armed robbery that had occurred some months before. Two hundred 'jurors' sentenced them to death. The trio could not plead in English, two being French and one Chilian. Vainly they called for an interpreter, for their cries were drowned by the yells of the now infuriated mob . . . the wagon was drawn from under them, and they were launched into eternity.

▲ A description of a lynching in San Francisco in the 1850s. It was written by Edward Buffum, a journalist, who had gone West in search of gold.

Territorial officials

- A **US Marshal** appointed by the President. He was responsible for the whole territory. Obviously, this was much too large an area for one man to control. It also took time to travel across the territory, although the coming of the railroad after 1869 helped. So the US Marshal appointed **Deputies**.
- **Deputy Marshals** worked more closely with the counties and towns to enforce federal law (laws passed by Congress). Their duties also included tracking down army deserters.
- **Town Marshals** were appointed locally in the townships. Their job was mostly to deal with local outbreaks of violence such as pub brawls or gambling disputes. They also could appoint Deputies.
- **Sheriffs** were responsible for law and order in the **counties**. They were usually elected for two years by the local people. Again, they were allowed to appoint under-sheriffs and deputies to help them. The latter did most of the work. Local people could also be called in to form a **posse** if criminals had to be chased. Some sheriffs behaved very responsibly but, because there was a need for a sheriff or town marshal to carry a gun, these officers were sometimes rather dubious characters.
- **Judges** (three) were appointed by the President to try cases. But these judges had to travel around the whole territory. Sometimes prisoners had to wait a long time for the judge to arrive. This made it very difficult for officers to stop **lynchings** (hangings without trial).

Legendary Lawmen

Wyatt Earp

Wyatt Earp was born in 1848 and died in 1929. He had a very mixed career. He started off as a buffalo hunter and a horse thief before becoming a lawman in the cow town of Wichita. He was dismissed from that job for fighting and moved on to Dodge City where he worked intermittently as a deputy marshal between 1875 and 1879. He is best remembered for the 'Gunfight at the O.K. Corral' in Tombstone, Arizona in 1881. There, according to legend, with his brothers Virgil and Morgan he overcame the 'bad guys', the Clantons and McLaurys, against all the odds. In fact, the evidence suggests that the three men who died were unarmed and shot in cold blood. The following year, when Morgan Earp was killed, Wyatt tracked down and killed the men that he suspected of murdering him. Amid such violence, it is amazing that he lived to be eighty !

James Butler, 'Wild Bill' Hickok

Hickok is another western legend. Born in 1837 he is remembered as a scout and a fighter of Indians, as well as a gunman. Hickok is supposed to have killed a hundred men although only seven are documented. He served as marshal in Abilene in the year that the cowmen were banned from the town. He always appeared well dressed and intimidating with his Colt Navy revolvers stuck in his gunbelt. He was eventually sacked from his job in Abilene after accidentally shooting one of his own Deputies. He once gave a young deputy a piece of advice, 'If you shoot a man, shoot him in the guts near the navel. You may not make a fatal shot, but he will get a shock that will paralyse his brain and arm so much that the fight is all over.' Hickok was shot in the back of the head by a hired killer in 1876.

Bill Tilghman

Tilghman was one example of a number of lawmen who, in spite of being poorly paid, devoted themselves to enforcing the law and carried out their jobs in a professional way. Before becoming a lawman he had been a buffalo hunter and had a reputation as a crack shot. He was a very intelligent and crafty man who would relentlessly chase criminals and use disguise if necessary to trap them. He was not a 'trigger-happy' lawman but would use persuasion to get his man to surrender. He was a Marshal in Dodge City before becoming Deputy US Marshal in Oklahoma. He rounded up three of the most notorious gangs of robbers – the Doolins, the Dalton Gang and the Starr Gang.

Source C

The cow town marshals and their deputies deserve the fame that clings to them to this day. Their characters varied from admirable to questionable and downright bad, but the best of them replaced anarchy and sometimes terror with the rule of law.

◀ **From Robin May, *The Story of the Wild West*, 1978.**

QUESTION

Study Source C and the information about the lawmen on this page. In what ways do these three lawmen illustrate the points that are made in Source C?

It was not unusual for totally unscrupulous men to become lawmen in order to further their own dishonest ends. A very good example was **Henry Plummer**. Plummer appeared to be an honest, law-abiding citizen. He was elected sheriff of Bannack in Montana in 1864. This was a gold-mining town. In fact, Plummer was the leader of a hundred strong band of robbers who called themselves 'The Innocents'. He used his new role as a cover for the fact that his men were robbing stage-coaches and committing other violent crimes. Plummer was eventually caught and hung by **vigilantes**.

Other methods of law enforcement

The Texas Rangers were set up by the Mexicans in 1820 when Texas was still Mexican territory. This was a small army of lawmen who proved to be very successful in keeping order in Texas where they were feared as well as respected. A similar band of Rangers was set up in Arizona.

Vigilance Committees were set up in some towns to keep law and order in the absence of a Marshal. Vigilantes (groups who took it upon themselves to enforce some kind of order) struck terror into the hearts of many because of their violent tactics. In some regions, they did successfully clean up the territory even though they paid only lip service to the law and often hanged the wrong person. But in others they used their position to settle private disputes and quarrels. Vigilantes were found in the new gold-mining towns in Montana and Nevada in the 1850s and 1860s and were involved in land disputes on the open range in the early 1890s (see also page 34).

Who dealt with disorder in the mining camps?

The discovery of gold in California in 1848 (see Chapter 2) was followed by further discoveries in Montana and Nevada in the 1860s and 1870s. This created the same kind of problems that had occurred in the earlier settlements in California. Gamblers, prostitutes, claim jumpers (people who stole other prospectors' claims to gold mines and often killed them in the process) and thieves were lured by the promise of gold. These camps became wild and desperate places. It took time for the federal authorities to send Marshals to these remote areas. So the miners organized themselves into **miners' courts** to deal with disorder. But these courts could deal effectively only with arguments between the miners themselves. Acts of theft, murder and violence committed by 'outsiders' were dealt with by the vigilante groups.

Trouble in Abilene

Once a year cow towns were 'invaded' by cowboys at the end of the long drive. After weeks on the trail, the cowboys were

Source D

To watch, pursue, and bring to justice the outlaws infesting the city, through the regularly constituted courts, if possible, through more summary courts, if necessary . . . no thief, burglar, incendiary, or assassin, shall escape punishment, either by quibbles of the law, the insecurity of prisons, the carelessness or corruption of the police, or a laxity of those who pretend to administer justice.

▲ The declaration of the first Committee of Vigilance of San Francisco in 1851.

Source E

A general lawlessness prevails through all these territories [Montana, Idaho, Colorado, Utah] resolving itself in the form of these [Vigilante] organizations; and everywhere they have brought trouble upon the community . . . The remedy for existing evils is greater than the evils.

▲ A criticism of vigilante activity from the editor of the *Idaho World* in 1865.

QUESTIONS

1 Read Source E. What is the writer saying about the vigilantes?

2 From what you have read and using Sources B and D, do you agree with this view? Explain your answer.

Source G

I have been in a good many towns but Newton is the fastest one I have ever seen. Here you may see young girls not over sixteen drinking whisky, smoking cigars, cursing, swearing . . . one of their townsmen says that . . . if I had any money then I would not be safe with it here. It is a common expression that they have a man every morning for breakfast.

▲ A description of the cow town of Newton, at the end of the Santa Fe railway, by a writer in the *Wichita Tribune*, July 1871.

Source H

His diet is principally Navy plug and whisky, and the occupation of his heart is gambling. . . . He generally wears a revolver on each side, which he will use with as little hesitation on a man as on a wild animal. Such a character is dangerous and desperate, and each one, generally, has killed his man. . . . .They drink, swear, and fight; and life with them is a round of boisterous gaiety and indulgence in sensual pleasure.

▲ An extract from the *Daily Commonwealth* a newspaper in Topeka, 1871, describing the cowboy.

desperate for relaxation and entertainment. Their high spirits gave the towns of Abilene, Dodge City and Newton particularly bad reputations for gambling and gunfights, although modern historians suggest that the number of murders committed in these towns has been greatly exaggerated. As in the mining towns, very little could be done about the disorder until the population was big enough for the people to have some form of local government. In Abilene, for example, it was not until 1870 that a mayor was elected. He then appointed a Town Marshal to 'clean up' the town. The man chosen was **Tom Smith**. He managed to halt guns being brought into the town but this did not stop the violence. Smith was killed by a settler and replaced by **'Wild Bill' Hickok**. The cowboys were finally banned from Abilene in 1872. By the 1880s, the cow towns had earned the reputation of being some of the wildest places in the West.

Gunslingers and gangs

The careers of lawmen such as Wyatt Earp make it clear that the differences between those who kept the law and those who broke it were often very blurred. Stories of the American West are full of gunmen who became sheriffs or Marshals and Marshals or sheriffs who became gunmen. The vast open spaces of the West and the difficulties of travelling, especially before the railroads, were an open invitation to people who wanted to rob and murder. There were plenty of these and they probably contributed the most to the lawlessness of the West and its legend. Back in the East, stories of the exploits of men like **Butch Cassidy** and the **Sundance Kid**, **Jesse James** and **Billy the Kid** captured the public imagination even while

▲ John Wesley Hardin (1853–95). Hardin was a typical 'badman' from Texas. A hardened killer (see page 55) he boasted he had killed 44 men when the Rangers finally caught up with him in 1878. He only just escaped from Marshall Bill Hickok in Abilene after shooting a man bacause he snored. His autobiography is probably authentic and worth reading.

▲ This picture of Billy the Kid is believed to a true likeness (undated). Billy the Kid is very much part of the legendary West. His actual identity is unknown for certain. His real name was either Henry McCarthy or William H Bonney. His career of crime began when he was 18 years old and in the Army when he shot and killed a blacksmith. He escaped from prison and became a hired gun in Lincoln County. His romanticised reputation came about because he claimed to have killed 21 men by the time he was 21 years old! He was hunted down by 'legendary lawman' Pat Garrett, who ambushed him on 14 July 1881. In reality, 'Billy the Kid' was probably responsible for the deaths of only four men.

▶ The Wild Bunch. From left to right, Harry Longbaugh ('The Sundance Kid'), William Carver, Ben Kilpatrick, Harvey Logan and Robert Parker ('Butch Cassidy'). The Wild Bunch were a gang of cattle rustlers led by Robert Parker and Harry Longbaugh. Like other gangs of the time, such as the James Younger gang (led by Jesse James) and the Dalton Gang, they turned their hands to bank and train robbery. Butch Cassidy and the Sundance Kid probably died in a shoot out in South America in 1909.

they were still alive. They were turned into romantic heroes in 'dime novels' and magazines.

Lawless ladies

Some notorious women were also associated with crimes of violence. One of the most famous was **Belle Starr** (1848–89) who came to be known as the 'Bandit Queen'. She had a fatal weakness for gunslingers and gangsters. She lived for a time with Cole Younger and then married a cattle rustler called Jim Reed. Later she married Sam Starr, a Cherokee outlaw. She planned and carried out robberies and rustled cattle and horses. She was the first woman in the West to be charged with horse-theft, which was a very serious crime. For these crimes she served a five year prison sentence before being shot in the back in 1889.

Etta Place, partner of the 'Sundance Kid' also took part in bank raids and train robberies with him and Butch Cassidy. **Annie McDougal** ('Cattle Annie') and **Jennie Metcalf** ('Little Breeches') were involved in almost every sort of crime. They sold whisky to the Indians, rustled horses and cattle, and carried out train and bank robberies. They were eventually arrested and sent to a reform school to be punished.

Why did cattlemen and homesteaders clash?

None of the new settlers in the West escaped from lawlessness in some shape or form. On the Plains, the homesteaders and the cattlemen came into conflict for a variety of reasons:
- Until the invention of barbed wire, there was nothing to protect the homesteaders' crops from the cattle that roamed freely on the open range.
- There were arguments over access to water as the homesteaders tried to stop the herds of Longhorns from crossing their land.
- When the cattlemen tried to establish their ranches on the Plains from the 1870s, there were arguments about land ownership.

Source L

▲ Belle Starr with one of her husbands, 'Blue Duck'. This photograph was taken later in her life.

QUESTIONS

1 In what ways were the mining and cow towns similar?

2 In what ways were they different?

3 According to Sources G and H (page 76), why were the cow towns so violent?

4 Why was it so difficult to establish law and order in the mining and cow towns?

5 Why do you think the gangs and gunslingers have been given romantic images ?

6 Were they really attractive characters?

All these disputes often became violent . In addition, before townships were established, remote homesteads and ranches were in danger from passing gangs of villains or from 'claim jumpers' who killed and stole their right to the land. This was especially true in Oklahoma where people 'rushed' to stake a claim to free land in 1889. They, in turn, were also in a dangerous position until their claim to the land was finally registered.

The **Johnson County War** of 1892 showed just how serious such conflicts as these could become. Although this took place in 1892, trouble had been brewing for several years.

Holding Down A Lot In Guthrie

▲ **This is a photograph of farmers who staked a claim to land at Guthrie, Oklahoma in 1889. It was former Indian land and the population of Guthrie went from 0 to 10,000 on the day of the Oklahoma Land Rush.**

7.2 The Johnson County War

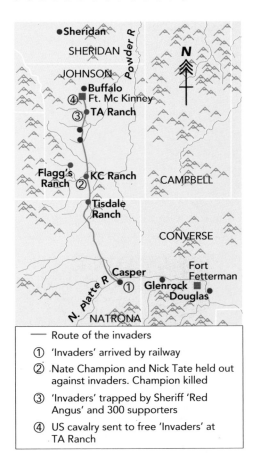

— Route of the invaders
① 'Invaders' arrived by railway
② Nate Champion and Nick Tate held out against invaders. Champion killed
③ 'Invaders' trapped by Sheriff 'Red Angus' and 300 supporters
④ US cavalry sent to free 'Invaders' at TA Ranch

▲ **Johnson County in the state of Wyoming in 1892.**

Johnson County was in Wyoming, a region of the High Plains. During the 1860s and 1870s, when farmers began to move on to the Plains, this area was avoided at first. This was partly because there was fierce resistance by the Indians to white settlement. But the cattlemen set up ranches in Wyoming in the 1870s and were firmly established there by the 1880s when the farmers came. Some of them had become wealthy and were trying to occupy more and more territory across the Plains. In Wyoming, these cattle 'barons' had formed themselves into the **Wyoming Stock Growers Association**. It had a membership of around a hundred cattlemen who met at the Cheyenne Club. They were a powerful force in the county. In 1890 Wyoming became a State. This strengthened the position of the cattle barons as the State Governor and a number of senators (members of the state assembly) joined the Cheyenne Club and supported the big ranchers.

In the process of acquiring more land, the barons came up against farmers and small cattle ranchers who resisted them and refused to give up their land. These farmers were accused of rustling cattle – a hanging offence. Although it is likely that some of them really were rustlers, this proved a very convenient way of removing resistance, especially as 'justice' was in the hands of vigilantes who worked for the barons.

Source A

An artist's impression of the lynching of Ella Watson and James Averill in Johnson County in 1889.

How did the 'war' begin ?

To answer this question, we need to go back to 1889. **A. J. Bothwell**, a rancher, wanted to take over some land that belonged to a storekeeper called **James Averill**. He lived on the land with a prostitute called **Ella Watson**. Averill accused Bothwell of being a 'land-grabber' and Bothwell, in turn, accused Averill of stealing cattle. Ella and James were lynched in front of their cabin. Neither Bothwell nor the lynchers was brought to trial.

What happened in the war?

In 1892 the Wyoming barons decided to bring in hired guns to sort out the 'rustlers' once and for all. A vigilante army of Texas gunmen was hired under the command of Major Frank Wolcott. The Union Pacific Railway even offered them transport from Texas ! The 'invaders' planned to capture Buffalo, the county town and kill the sheriff, 'Red' Angus. They cut the telegraph wires to isolate Johnson County from the outside world. However, they had been seen attacking the KC Ranch on the way to Buffalo, and 'Red' Angus gathered an army of farmers and small ranchers and forced the vigilante army back to its base at the TA Ranch and laid seige to the ranch. The barons used their political connections to call in the US Cavalry who eventually freed them. In spite of what the papers reported at the time, it was an almost bloodless war. The victims were Nate Champion and Nick Tate, the two alleged rustlers who had held out at the KC Ranch.

The barons did not have to answer for their actions in a court of law. But when news of the Johnson County War spread, their behaviour was generally condemned. The cattle barons were never allowed so much power and influence again. The homesteaders continued to farm in Wyoming and the cattlemen fenced in their ranches. It was the end of the open range.

Source B

An undated photograph of Ella Watson.

Source C

An undated photograph of James Averill.

QUESTIONS

1 Look carefully at Sources A, B and C. How much of Source A is accurate? Use your knowledge and the Sources to answer the question.

2 Is the artist in Source A sympathetic towards Ella and James? Explain your answer.

7.3 The end of the 'wild' West

By 1895 the problems of lawlessness in the West were gradually being resolved. There were several reasons for this:

- The expansion of the railways after 1869 made it easier for US Marshals and judges to enforce the law. The development of the **telegraph** also helped communications.
- As more and more families moved westwards there was a greater demand for the law to be kept. Settlers had moved to find prosperity and a better life, so they were not prepared to tolerate lawlessness. The banning of the cowboys from Abilene in 1872 is an example of this.
- As more and more territories became States (see map) they took on responsibility for keeping law and order. Important decisions no longer had to be made hundreds of miles away.
- As State and local government, such as town councils, became established, the surroundings in which people lived were improved. The shanty towns were replaced by properly planned towns with roads, sanitation, water supplies and better quality buildings. A civilized environment helped to encourage civilized behaviour.

	States by 1890
•	Town with 5,000 to 100,000 inhabitants
o	Town with over 100,000 inhabitants

▲ **The western states of the United States of America by 1890.**

However, even in the 1890s it was still possible for law and order to break down. The Johnson County War is proof of this.

But, by 1895, the frontier had disappeared. There was hardly any area west of the Mississippi that did not now contain white settlers. It was a triumph for 'manifest destiny'. But the victory was won at a huge cost and the price had to be paid by the people who were in truth the first Americans – the Native Indians.

7.4 EXERCISE

1 Explain in as much detail as possible how each of the following contributed to the development of law and order:
  a vigilante groups
  b miners' courts
  c the US Government
  d US Marshals, county sheriffs and town marshals
  e the railways
  f settlers and their families
  g local government

2 Why was there lawlessness in the West? Answer in as much detail as possible.

3 Was there law and order in the West by 1895? Explain your answer.

4 'The romantic images of the 'wild' West make it difficult for us to imagine what a terrifying place it must have been.'
  a In what ways was the West terrifying?
  b Which groups of people would you say suffered the most as a result of lawlessness?
  c Do you agree with this statement? Explain your answer.

CHAPTER 8

HOW THE PLAINS WERE WON AND LOST

'The last gunfire on the Great Plains between Indians and soldiers of the United States was exchanged on a bitterly cold day in 1890. . . . On that day, on Wounded Knee Creek in South Dakota, a forlorn and hungry band of Sioux, including women and children, was goaded and frightened into making a gesture of resistance to Army authority. When it was over, the Indian wars of the Plains were ended and with them the long struggle of all the American Indians . . . to preserve some portion of their ancestral lands and tribal ways.

Ralph K. Andrist, _The Long Death_, 1964.

The long struggle between the Plains Indians and the settlers that ended with the **Battle of Wounded Knee** had been going on since the 1840s when the first settlers went West. This chapter is about this struggle, why it started and ended so disastrously for the Indians.

8.1 Why did the Indians go on the warpath ?

Wherever white settlers went in the West, the lifestyle of the Native Indians was disrupted and almost destroyed. This did not mean that all the Indians went on the warpath. Some, such as the Nez Perce in Oregon and the Utes in Colorado, placidly accepted their fate. On the Plains, however, the more forceful tribes such as the Sioux, Cheyennes and Arapaho fiercely defended their lands and culture. This is not surprising, since in 1832, the Great Plains had been given by the US Government to all the Indian tribes as their land. The eastern edge of the Plains was established as a **Permanent Indian Frontier** after the tribes that lived in the Mississippi valley had been moved West, making the Plains a huge Indian reservation.

The invasion of the Plains

Contact with white people was not entirely new to the native Indians in the 1840s. For some time, they had traded animal skins with them, they had drunk their whisky and had been infected with their diseases. When the first settlers crossed on the Oregon Trail the Indians were not immediately alarmed. As more and more settlers came and when gold was discovered in California (in 1848) the impact on the Indians was destructive. The travellers 'invaded' Indian land, shot the buffalo and in 1849 brought cholera to the Plains. From the 1860s onwards the Indians moved into ever decreasing areas

Source A

They are in terrible want of food half the year. The travel upon the road [trail] drives the buffalo off or else confines them to a narrow path during the period of migration. . . . Their women are pinched with want and their children are constantly crying with hunger.

▲ **Thomas Fitzpatrick, the Indian Agent for the US Government in the Upper Platte and Arkansas River Country describing the Indian tribes. He was reporting to the Government in 1853, on the effect of the wagon trains on the Oregon Trail crossing Indian land.**

▲ A painting by Oscar Berninghaus (1874–1952) called *Indians Watching the Wagon Train*.

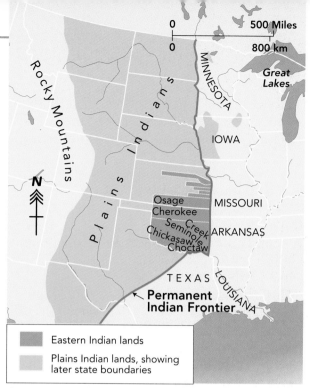

Eastern Indian lands

Plains Indian lands, showing later state boundaries

▲ The permanent Indian frontier and Indian lands on the Great Plains.

as land on the Plains was opened up for settlement by the Government. The fundamental differences in the beliefs and way of life of the Indians and the white settlers (see Chapter 2) made it impossible for them to live side by side and it is not surprising that the Indians felt driven to protect what they believed to be theirs by right.

Army incompetence

Indian attacks on wagon trains in the early days and later, on lonely homesteads horrified and angered settlers. They thought that these attacks were entirely unprovoked. The Government sent units of the US army to protect travellers. The tension and suspicion grew so great that the slightest incident could spark off a major confrontation which could lead to massacre. Army officers often showed ignorance as well as insensitivity in their dealings with the Indians.

Broken treaties

By 1851 the Indians had already been identified as a 'problem'. In Washington, the politicians decided that the solution was to negotiate with the Indians. This was difficult because the bands and chiefs within each tribe had a lot of independence and did not always agree to keep to agreements. The Government wanted to create territories for the settlers so it had to persuade the Indians to agree to live in a smaller area, and accept

compensation of supplies of food and clothing, so if there were no buffalo nearby, they would not die. It was agreed that the newly allocated lands would not be entered by white settlers. Major treaties were signed with the Indians at Fort Laramie in 1851 and 1868 (see page 84). These were broken almost before the ink had dried on the page. Long before 1868, the Indians had realized that white people could not be trusted. By this time, the Government had come up with a new policy of concentrating the Indians on even smaller areas called **reservations**. This meant that the culture and way of life of the Indians, as well as their dignity and self-respect, were threatened. If they wanted to survive the only way was to fight.

QUESTIONS

1 Look at Source B. Why do you think the Indians watching the wagon train?

2 In what ways does Source A help you to understand the purpose of the painting?

3 Do you think the artist sympathetic towards the Indians? Explain your answer.

There were four 'wars' between the Indians and US soldiers between 1855 and 1868, although small scale skirmishes and attacks on settlers persisted throughout this period. These were:

- **1862** Little Crow's War (Sioux)
- **1863** The Cheyenne Uprising
- **1867** Red Cloud's War (Sioux)
- **1868** The 'Winter Campaign' against the Cheyenne.

1862 Little Crow's War

Little Crow was the chief of the Santee Sioux, part of the Sioux nation. His 'war' was really a revolt against reservations. His people had given up their homelands and agreed to move to a reservation in Minnesota. Life on the reservation was hard. In 1861 the crops failed and the compensation allowance they had been promised did not arrive from Washington. About 12,000 people faced starvation. The authorities on the reservation treated their protests and demands for food with contempt (see Source A). Little Crow was angry because he had tried to keep to the terms of the treaty and had been made to look a coward in the eyes of his tribe. So, in August 1862, the Santee Sioux attacked the white traders and settlers who lived in the **Agency** (the organization set up by the government to run the reservation). Twenty men were killed and ten women and children were captured. They took all the food and provisions from the warehouses and burned all the agency buildings. Later they ambushed a party of soldiers coming to deal with the incident.

The attacks on settlers and on the army continued for almost three months before the army finally rounded up the rebellious Indians. Of the 307 Santees who were tried for the uprising, 38 were hanged. Little Crow was later shot by a settler. The following year, the remaining 2,000 of his people were moved to a new, even smaller reservation in Missouri. Here the conditions were even worse and several hundred of the Santee died during the first winter.

The Cheyenne uprising of 1863

The hardships of life on the reservations also sparked off disturbances amongst the Cheyenne. Under the terms of the Fort Wise Treaty of 1861, their chief, **Black Kettle**, who was a peaceful man, had agreed to move his people onto the Sand Creek Reservation in Colorado. In that year, Colorado was opened up for white settlement. The land in the reservation was dry and infertile and made it impossible for the Indians to survive there.

Treaties with the Indians

Fort Laramie Treaty 1851
- *defined the Indian homelands.*
- *promised the Indians that settlers would not enter these lands.*
- *gave the Indians food, clothing, cattle and equipment for ten years as compensation for loss of land. This was reduced to five years, and in 1854 the Indian lands were reduced still further.*

Fort Wise Treaty 1861
Sand Creek Reservation set up in Colorado for the Cheyenne. It was very poor quality land.

Medicine Creek Treaty 1867
The Cheyennes, Arapahoes, Commanches and Kiowas agreed to give up their land and move to small reservations in the south-east of the Plains.

Fort Laramie Treaty 1868
Redefined the territory of the Sioux nation. It included the Black Hills of Dakota.

Source A

If they are hungry, let them eat grass or their own dung.

▲ The response of Andrew Myrick, a trader, on hearing that the Santee were starving. Myrick was murdered in the attack on the agency. His mouth had been stuffed with grass.

1876 Battle of the Little Bighorn – Custer and the 7th Cavalry wiped out by Sitting Bull, Crazy Horse and the Sioux.

1862 Little Crow's War – revolt by Santee Sioux against bad conditions on reservations.

Indian territory

1867 Red Cloud's War – Sioux attacked travellers on Bozeman trail. Red Cloud forced withdrawal of army. Destroyed forts on the trail.

1890 Wounded Knee – final defeat of Sioux. Big Foot's band destroyed by army. Sioux forced to live on reservations.

All Indians located on reservations across America.

1863-4 Cheyenne uprising – Response to hardships on reservations. Starving Cheyennes attacked wagon trains for food. Army launched attack on Black Kettle's village at Sand Creek.

Blackfoot

C A N A D A

Atsina

Flathead
Kutenai

Sioux

Crow

Sioux

Chippewa

Northern Cheyenne

Battle of the Little Bighorn

Sioux

Sioux

Shoshoni

Arapaho

Sioux

N

Wounded Knee

Ute

Battle of Sand Creek

Battle of Washita

M E X I C O

Indian Territory

0 ——— 500 Miles
0 ——— 800 km

▲ The main clashes between the Indians and the US army between 1860 and 1890.

1868 Winter Campaign – Army campaign against Cheyennes. Custer and Sheridan attacked Black Kettle's village on the Washita.

Source B

We have waited a long time. We have no food, but here are stores filled with food. We ask you to make some arrangement by which we can get food, or we will keep ourselves from starving.

▲ A comment made by Little Crow, who had kept to the terms of the treaty of 1861.

Source C

I ordered the men to commence killing them. . . . They lost . . . some twenty-six killed and thirty wounded. . . . I burnt up their lodges and everything I could.

▲ Major Jacob Downing who led the attack on the Cheyenne village in Cedar Canyon in 1864.

Source D

You have no idea of the uncontrollable panic everywhere in this country. The most horrible massacres have been committed; children nailed alive to trees . . . women violated . . . everything that horrible ingenuity could devise.

▲ General John Pope of the US army describing attacks on settlers by Little Crow's tribe.

They continued to roam in the area in search of buffalo or other game. But in 1863 there was none to be found. Faced with starvation, the Cheyenne began to attack wagon trains. However, they only stole food. The travellers were left unharmed. The plight of the Cheyennes failed to arouse any sympathy from the army. In 1864 news came that they were stealing cattle. So the army mounted an attack on one of their villages in **Cedar Canyon**. It is clear that the purpose of the attack was to punish the Indians. Black Kettle's peace parties, sent to negotiate, were gunned down. The village was wiped out.

Enter Colonel Chivington

At this point the responsibility for protecting settlers and dealing with the Indians was given to **Colonel John M. Chivington**. He was one of many officers whose aim was to kill as many Indians as possible. The army decided that tribes wishing for peace should report to army forts. The Cheyenne reported to Chivington who chose to misinterpret Black Kettle's peace move.

Massacre at Sand Creek

At dawn, on 29 November 1864, Chivington's men attacked Black Kettle's camp at Sand Creek. The chief's attempts to raise the American flag and the white flag of peace were ignored. The Indians were not only killed but their bodies were also horribly mutilated. While accurate figures of the dead were impossible to obtain, it seems certain that at least 163 Cheyennes were killed, of whom 110 were women and children. Those taken prisoner were shown to white American theatre audiences during the interval along with the scalps of their dead. This incident became known as the Sand Creek Massacre – it was one of the worst atrocities in the history of the West. When news of the massacre reached the East it was not welcomed and Chivington realised he could be facing the possibility of a court martial. He left the army to avoid this, his hopes of political advancement ruined.

Sand Creek – battle or massacre ?

Source E

Black Kettle ran from his lodge shouting. . . . Then, in a withering blast, cannon and rifle fire swept through the camp. Few of the Cheyennes had arms or any opportunity to obtain them because the first overwhelming charges drove them away from their lodges. . . Here and there, braves with weapons attempted to make stands in hollows or pits in the creek bank to protect women and children.

▲ Ralph K. Andrist, The Long Death, 1964.

Source F

Some thirty or forty squaws, collected in a hole for protection . . . sent out a little girl about six years old with a white flag on a stick. She was shot and killed. . . . I saw quite a number of infants in arms killed by their mothers.

▲ From an eyewitness account by Robert Bent, a half-cast Cheyenne, who was in Black Kettle's camp that day. His sickening description of what he saw was supported by some of the soldiers own accounts of their own exploits.

Source G

It looked too hard for me to see little children on their knees begging for their lives, having their brains beaten out like dogs.

▲ Captain Silas Soule who was present at the attack, but refused to order his men to fire on the Indians.

Source H

At daylight this morning I attacked a Cheyenne village of . . . .about nine hundred to a thousand warriors. We killed . . . between four and five hundred. All died nobly.

▲ Chivington's report of his achievements immediately after the attack.

▲ Chivington and his men attack Black Kettle's camp at Sand Creek. A Painting by Robert Lindreux in 1936.

Source J

All acquitted themselves well. Colorado soldiers have again covered themselves with glory.

▲ From a report of the Sand Creek Massacre in the *Denver News*.

Source K

I never saw more bravery displayed by any set of people on the face of the earth than by these Indians.

▲ Major Anthony, a US cavalryman, who was present at the massacre.

QUESTIONS

1 **a** Study Sources E to G. Write a description of what happened at Sand Creek using these sources.

b From what you know about the circumstances surrounding the incident at Sand Creek and the information that you have been given about Sources E to G, are you satisfied that he description you have written is accurate? Explain your answer using your knowledge.

2 Read Sources H to K. Why are they suggesting such a different version of the events? Use your knowledge to explain your answer.

3 Was Sand Creek a battle or a massacre? Use your knowledge about the incident as well as the sources to explain your answer carefully. You might also consider whether you have sufficient reliable evidence here to reach a decision.

What happened after Sand Creek?

Black Kettle managed to escape the carnage in his village. He continued to work for peace, but the massacre had violent consequences. The Sioux, Arapaho, Kiowa and Comanche Indians joined forces with the Cheyennes and attacks on white settlements escalated into a war which lasted until 1868 and cost the US Government $30,000,000. The hostilities spread from Colorado eastwards into Kansas and Nebraska and westwards into Minesota. Hundreds of settlers were affected either by direct attacks or by having to abandon their homesteads for safety. The Indians were now even deadlier enemies because, in addition to their skills of fighting on horseback, they had guns. On the other hand, the railway helped the army to move across the Plains more rapidly.

In 1867 the Cheyennes, Comanches, Kiowas and Arapahoes made peace at **Medicine Lodge Creek** and agreed to leave their hunting grounds and settle permanently on small reservations which they would not leave. Weary of warfare, they had accepted that they could not resist the white settlers and that the reservations would end their traditional way of life. But **Red Cloud**, chief of the Oglala Sioux refused to admit defeat.

Red Cloud's War 1867

When the Homestead Act was passed in 1862, migration on to the Plains had been slow. That same year, gold was discovered in the Rocky Mountains in Montana. This resulted in another rush of gold diggers and created the need for a trail to link the new gold fields with the Oregon Trail. This was established by a gold miner called John Bozeman and so became known as the **Bozeman Trail** (see map). Unfortunately, the trail passed through the hunting grounds of the Sioux. Red Cloud was determined to resist this intrusion into his territory which had been guaranteed by the Fort Laramie Treaty of 1851. As a result, travellers were regularly attacked by the Sioux. By 1866 the US Government decided to take action. Talks were set up with Red Cloud but, at the same time, the army, under Colonel Carrington, was ordered to build a line of forts along the trail to protect travellers. Red Cloud was furious. He withdrew from the talks and began to attack the soldiers and workers insisting that there would be no peace until they were gone from his land. He was joined by two other equally determined Sioux leaders, **Crazy Horse** and **Sitting Bull** (see page 5).

In December 1866, a detachment of soldiers under **Captain Fetterman** left Fort Philip Kearny to protect woodcutters building the fort. They were lured into an ambush by the Sioux. Fetterman and about a 100 soldiers were killed. So, in the spring of 1867, the Government agreed to withdraw the army from the area and abandon the forts. These were burnt to the ground by the Indians as the soldiers retreated.

Red Cloud's victory ?

It seemed like a victory for Red Cloud and the Sioux. But it was only temporary. The massacre of Fetterman and the humiliating retreat only increased the determination of officers in the army to deal once and for all with the Indians.

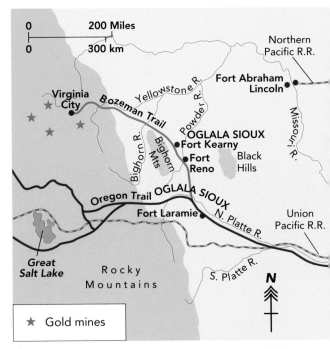

▲ **The Bozeman Trail and the line of forts built by the army.**

◀ A painting by Schreyvogel of the battle of Washita showing the attack at dawn by Custer's 7th cavalry.

Source **M**

I do not understand how the massacre of Fetterman's party could have been so complete. . . . We must act with vindictive earnestness against the Sioux, even to their extermination, men, women and children.

▲ General William Tecumseh Sherman, who was in charge of military operations on the Plains, in 1868.

Source **N**

If a white man commits murder and robs, we hang him or send him to the penitentiary [prison]; if an Indian does the same, we have been in the habit of giving him more blankets.

▲ General Philip Sheridan at the outset of the 'Winter Campaign'. Sheridan, like Sherman and Chivington before him, saw no alternative to the Indian problem but to exterminate them.

Fort Laramie Treaty 1868

As for Red Cloud, he enjoyed his victory until November of 1868, when he finally agreed to the terms of the Fort Laramie Treaty. This created the Great Sioux Reservation which included **Bighorn Mountains** and the **Black Hills of Dakota**, areas which were sacred to the Sioux. White settlers were not allowed to enter these lands. Unfortunately, not all of the Sioux bands agreed to these terms. Young chieftains such as Crazy Horse and Sitting Bull refused to live within the confined space of the reservation. Here were the seeds of future conflict.

The 'Winter Campaign' 1868

By 1868 the US army had begun to understand Indian attitudes to warfare more clearly. They realized, for example, that they never fought in winter. So, in 1868, when some of the Cheyennes in Kansas and Nebraska renewed their attacks on settlers, it was decided to mount a winter campaign against them. Sherman recalled **George Armstrong Custer** to duty. Custer had been court-martialled and suspended from duty in 1867. Together with **General Philip Sheridan**, he mounted a surprise attack at dawn on Black Kettle's village on the Washita River – which became known as the **Battle of Washita**. Not all of the Cheyenne had been involved in the attacks on settlers and Black Kettle's village was flying the white flag to show that its people were peaceful. So this was almost a repeat of Sand Creek. Once again, the Indians were sleeping when the soldiers struck and had little time to organize any defence. Black Kettle and his wife were killed. The majority of the dead were women, children and the old. Custer was very pleased with his performance. The Cheyenne and their Arapaho, Kiowa and Comanche allies, returned to their reservations. The original treaty that they had signed at Medicine Creek had given them the right to come off the reservation to hunt buffalo. This right was now removed.

QUESTION

From what you have learned about the conflict with the Indians, how much were they to blame for what happened to them in these years? Explain your answer.

8.3 Conflicting attitudes to the Indian problem

Within the accounts of the Indian conflicts that you have studied there is some indication of the attitudes of white Americans towards the Indians. It is important to consider how they developed and changed during the period from about 1850 to 1868.

The Indians were identified as a 'problem' from the moment that settlers began to go West. The first response by the Government was to share out the land. So the Indian homelands were re-defined and the tribes had to accept smaller areas of land. This was the so-called policy of **concentration**. But the boundaries of these areas were not respected as more settlers arrived. As you have seen, this sent the Indians from some tribes onto the warpath.

Source A

They made us many promises, more than I can remember, but they never kept but one; they promised to take away our land and they took it.

▲ An elder of the Lakota Sioux.

Source B

There suddenly arose such a shout as is never heard unless upon some battlefield, a shout almost loud enough to raise the roof of the Opera House, 'Exterminate them ! Exterminate them !

▲ A report by Senator Doolittle of Wisconsin. He is describing the response of the audience to a speech he made about the treatment of the Indians in the Opera House, Denver, Colorado in 1865.

The 'exterminators'

After 1860 tribes such as the Cheyennes, Arapaho, Kiowas, Comanches and Sioux became more hostile. Divisions began to appear as to what should be done about the problem. People who were in the West – settlers, traders and army officers such as Chivington, Sherman and Sheridan made no secret of their belief that the Indians should be destroyed. This view became more widespread after the massacre of Fetterman and his troops in 1866. They wanted the government to hand over the Indian 'problem' to the US army. The exceptions to this view in the West were either those who had particularly taken the trouble to understand the Indians or the Indian agents. These were government officials who had been appointed to oversee the Indians. As they saw them at closer quarters, they tended to be more sympathetic to their situation.

The 'humanitarians'

In Washington, many politicians took a more **humanitarian** view. They believed that aggressive tactics would only make the Indians more hostile. To some extent, the events of the 1860s seemed to suggest that this view was correct. They insisted that the responsibility for Indian affairs should remain in the hands of the Department of the Interior and not the Army. Even so, the hostilities of the late 1860s made it clear that something more drastic would have to be done. The result was the establishment of small reservations. These, as you have seen, were accepted by the Indians at Medicine Creek (1867), at Fort Laramie (1868) and by many of the other, smaller tribes. At first, the Indians were allowed to leave the reservations to hunt the buffalo, but by the late 1860s this was no longer the case. Reservation life meant total dependency on the Government. President Grant, who had drawn up the policy, wanted the Indians to learn to live like white people and to abandon their tribal ways. To ensure this the Government ordered the systematic slaughter of the buffalo and by 1890 the buffalo had been almost completely exterminated.

▲ **General William Tecumseh Sherman.**

QUESTION

Explain how the two different attitudes towards the Indians developed between 1850 and 1868.

8.4 From the Little Bighorn to Wounded Knee

Why did the Sioux go back on the warpath?

Peace in the Great Sioux reservation and the Bighorn country, where Crazy Horse and Sitting Bull still roamed freely, remained only as long as the white settlers did not enter the territory.

In 1874 rumours were going around that there was gold to be found in the Black Hills of Dakota, the sacred land of the Sioux. By 1875 prospectors were pouring into the area. The terms of the Fort Laramie Treaty of 1868 were violated. In response to popular demand, Government officials tried to negotiate a price for the land with Red Cloud. But the other chiefs would not agree, particularly Crazy Horse and Sitting Bull. As Crazy Horse put it, 'One does not sell the land upon which the people walk'. Hostilities

were inevitable. In December 1875 the Sioux were ordered to return to the reservation. They were given 60 days to do so but they refused. This telegraph from President Grant made the outcome inevitable: 'Said Indians are hereby turned over to the War Department for such action as you may deem proper'. By the spring of 1876, the renegade Indians had gathered in a huge village in the valley of the Little Bighorn. It consisted of 1,000 tipis and about 7,000 people of whom 2,000 were warriors.

What were the army's plans ?

President Grant had clearly given the army the task of either rounding up the Indians or wiping them out. Once the Indians had been located, a three-pronged attack was planned (see map). The forces of **General Crook** advancing north from Fort Fetterman, were

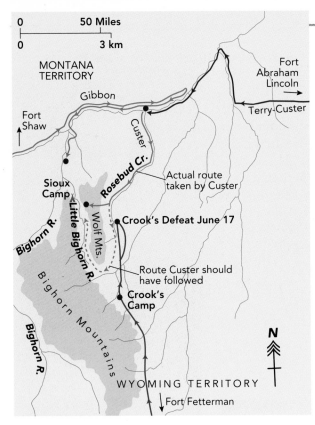

▲ The strategy of the Bighorn Campaign.

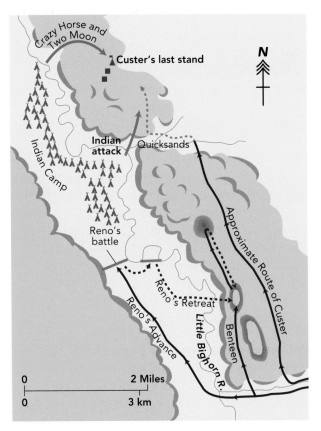

▲ The movements of Custer and his men at the Battle of the Little Bighorn.

engaged by the Sioux led by Crazy Horse. After a fierce battle, Crook decided to retreat. The task was left to **Colonel Gibbon**, advancing from Fort Shaw and **Generals Terry** and **Custer** coming from Fort Abraham Lincoln. Custer was to travel south along the Rosebud Creek and advance up the Bighorn Valley. He received strict instructions to wait for Gibbon and Terry before attacking the Indians. What followed became the legendary battle of the Indian Wars – the **Battle of the Little Bighorn**. It is dominated by the name of one man – **George Armstrong Custer**.

What happened at the Little Bighorn ?

Custer took with him about 600 men and two other officers – **Major Reno** and **Captain F. W. Benteen**. On 24 June Custer's Indian scouts told him that the village had been sighted and warned him that it was huge. They also said that there was not enough amunition to fight so many Indians.

Custer ignored all the warnings. He was elated at the prospect of defeating the Sioux and their allies and, in the process, getting all the glory for himself. He force-marched his men through the night from the Rosebud to the Bighorn River. They were ready to attack by the next morning. Custer had no intention of waiting. Perhaps he thought that the Indians might escape when they saw the soldiers. What he could not have known was that they were determined to stand and fight.

He used his usual tactics of splitting his men to surround the enemy. On this occasion it did not work. Reno and Benteen were sent up the Little Bighorn valley and came under attack from the Indians (see the plan). Custer continued to advance along the north bank but, when he tried to cross the river to attack the village, he was prevented from doing so by quicksands and was forced up on to the bluffs above the river. There he was easily spotted by the Sioux. More careful scouting of the territory might have avoided the catastrophe that followed. At some point, Custer was attacked by the Indians armed

with Winchester rifles. He and all his men were killed. No one lived to explain what happened and the only eye-witness accounts have come from the Indians.

▲ An unusual painting of the Battle of the Little Bighorn by William Herbert Dunton (1915). It shows the battle from the position of the Indians. Custer is on top of the hill on the right.

Was the Bighorn really a victory for the Indians?

In the short term, the answer must be 'yes'. News of Custer's defeat reached the East as the centenary celebrations were underway of the birth of the USA. It shocked the nation. But the army was now set on revenge:

Source **B**

- All Indian reservations were placed under military control.
- The renegade Sioux were rounded up and their territory was taken away from them. They were forced on to reservations.
- Crazy Horse finally surrendered in 1877. He was murdered as he was being taken into custody at Camp Robinson in Nebraska.
- All Indians, hostile or otherwise, from all over the continent, felt the effects of the army's anger as they were finally forced off what remained of their homelands and on to reservations elsewhere. So, for example, the Apaches with their great chief, Geronimo, and Chief Joseph with the Nez Perce from Oregon found themselves transported to Oklahoma.
- The Indians had to obey the laws of the USA instead of their own tribal laws.
- Sitting Bull escaped to Canada but later returned in 1885 to appear in Buffalo Bill's Wild West Show!

▲ One of the many photographs that Custer had taken of himself.

Reservation life and the Dawes Act 1887

Life on the reservations was very hard. Food supplies were poor. The buffalo had almost gone. The Government was in the process of breaking down tribal bonds by, amongst other things, dividing the land into allottments and allocating it on an individual basis. In 1887 the Government passed the **General Allotments Act**, known more commonly as the **Dawes Act**. This divided up much of the remaining Indian land into 160 acre allotments, some of which were given to Indian families. The rest went to white settlers. The Act was devastating for the Indian families. They had to learn how to be farmers. Many were eventually cheated out of their allocated land. By 1900, Indian land had been reduced from 155 million acres to 78 million. They were driven to poverty, drink and suicide. Meanwhile, the young braves became frustrated and demoralized. There were no more oppotunities to show their skills and courage. Their tribal culture no longer had meaning or reason.

And so to Wounded Knee

The revenge of the army was completed in 1890. The people were frightened by rumours of soldiers coming to kill them. In these circumstances they were an easy prey to a strange cult known as the **Ghost Dance**.

This began in Nevada where a Paiute Indian called **Wovoka** began to tell the people that a time was coming when the white people would leave the land and the Indian dead would return. Then they would recover their homelands and live as they had before. To bring this about they were told to perform the Ghost Dance. This would put them into contact with the Great Spirit. Sadly, it only made them restless and aggressive. This alarmed the authorities. The trouble reached a climax on the Pine Ridge reservation in Wounded Knee Creek in South Dakota. What happened seems uncertain. It appeared that soldiers attempting to disarm a band of Sioux led by Chief Big Foot were provoked and opened fire on the band, killing 153 men, women and children. It became known as the **Battle of Wounded Knee**. Some historians suggest that the army wanted to kill the Indians. Whatever the truth may be, it was the last act in a massive human tragedy.

Source C

The inevitable explosion happened at Wounded Knee Creek . . . when warriors under chief Big Foot provoked a bloody and destructive battle with soldiers who were disarming them.

▲ H.S. Commager, *The West*, 1984.

QUESTION

Read Source C and then look at the extract which opens Chapter 8. Are these two historians giving conflicting interpretations of the Battle of Wounded Knee? Explain your answer.

SUMMARY

▶ **1832** Permanent Indian Frontier established along the eastern edge of the Plains.

▶ **1840s** White settlers blazed the trails to the West; Indian tribes traded with Whites.

▶ **1848** The gold rush. Many more settlers disrupted the Indians' hunting.

▶ **1849** Cholera came to the Plains.

▶ **1861** Fort Wise Treaty.

▶ **1860s** Homesteaders and cattlemen took over more and more land on the Plains.

▶ **1862** Little Crow's War (Sioux).

▶ **1863** Cheyenne uprising. Battle of Sand Creek.

▶ **1866** Massacre of Fetterman and his troops.

▶ **1867** The Medicine Creek Treaty. Red Cloud's War (Sioux). Battle of Washita.

▶ **1868** The 'Winter Campaign'.

▶ **1876** Battle of the Little Bighorn.

▶ **1887** The Dawes Act.

▶ **1890** Battle of Wounded Knee.

The white Americans had finally won the West and the Indians had lost everything.

The 'closing of the frontier', 1890

By 1890 the United States of America stretched from the Atlantic to the Pacific. Although the population remained dense in the East, pockets of settlement had developed all over the continent. The frontier that had formed the limits of Western expansion had disappeared. In 1890, the director of the US Cencus Bureau announced that the frontier was closed. Only four territories remained and these were soon to become states. It seemed that the great era of pioneer expansion was drawing to a close. The American people had fulfilled their 'manifest destiny'.

8.5 EXERCISE

George Armstrong Custer – hero or glory hunter?

Custer has been both praised and blamed for the tragedy at the Little Bighorn. Was he a courageous soldier or did he sacrifice his men for his own glory ? Look carefully at the sources and try to form an opinion based on the evidence.

Background information

- Custer graduated at West Point Military Academy where he had a reputation for being slovenly and impulsive. He was placed last in his class.
- During the Civil War his courage and daring were valued. He became a Brigadier-General.
- He was completely devoted to his wife, Libby. In 1867 he deserted his post in the West and force-marched his men so that he could return to his wife. He was court-martialled for this and for the execution, without court martial, of twelve deserters from his troop.

Source 1

He was a flamboyant leader. He designed his own uniform which consisted of a wide-brimmed hat, trousers with a double stripe running down the seam, a sailor's wide-collared shirt, a red cravat, and on the sleeves of his jacket an intricate arabesque of interlacing loops of gold braid. Add to this the golden hair grown long and lying in ringlets on his shoulders and the man becomes rather overpowering in his gaudiness and glitter.

▲ R. K. Andrist, *The Long Death*, 1964.

Source 2

A man of supreme courage and boundless energy who had retained the enthusiasm of a youth at the cost of never quite attaining the judgement of a man.

▲ R. K. Andrist, *The Long Death*, 1964.

Source 3

I have never met a more enterprising, gallant or dangerous enemy during those four years of terrible war.

▲ Major General T L Rosser of the Confederate army (army of the southern states during the Civil War).

Source 4

A cold-blooded, untruthful, unprincipled man. He is universally despised by all the officers of his regiment.

▲ General Stanley. Custer served under him in a campaign against the Indians in 1872.

1 From your knowledge, do you think Andrist's interpretation fair (sources 1 and 2)?

2 a Look back at Source B on page 93 and read Sources 3 and 4.
   b Do they support the views expressed in Sources 1 and 2? Do they contradict these views?

3 Was Custer a hero or a glory hunter? You might also consider whether you have enough evidence and what other kinds of evidence you need.

INDEX